buildings, projects,
microarchitecture workshops

richard horden
architecture and teaching

edited by – herausgegeben von:
lehrstuhl für entwerfen und gebäudelehre
prof. richard horden, tu-münchen

birkhäuser verlag
basel · boston · berlin

architecture as methodology
architektur als methode

niccolò baldassini, who is an architect, journalist and aerospace engineer, won a competition at cranfield for long-duration flights with this lightweight design.

niccolò baldassini, architekt, journalist und luftfahrt-ingenieur, gewann mit diesem leichten entwurf in cranfield einen wettbewerb für langzeitflüge.

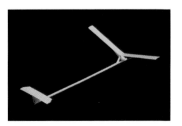

foreword

in 1984, the year in which the first yacht house was built, boatbuilding was dominated by aluminium technology. today, its place has been taken by composite materials. richard horden's architecture has continued to evolve parallel to these developments. his work is guided not by a blind passion for technology, but by the knowledge that technology can function in a synergetic way to bring man closer to nature – as horden has already demonstrated in his skihaus designs. improvements in the social sector are another area of concern, as can be seen in his st mark's hospital scheme. pursuing this line of thought, horden has made a number of innovative and quite specific contributions to architecture: he postulated the idea of energy transfer; he initiated the concept of microarchitecture; and finally, he introduced the science of aerodynamics into design and structural planning. this desire to reach out to new horizons has remained unchanged; and since 1996, he has accepted the challenge of communicating his knowledge to others. his intense commitment to teaching reveals itself in the quality of his students' work. horden's thinking is not based a priori on a certain aesthetic, but on a precise, informed methodology – the only fundamental value in architecture that can really be communicated and taught.

niccolò baldassini

1984, im baujahr des ersten yacht house, war im yachtbau die technologie des aluminiums vorherrschend, heute sind es die kompositmaterialien. parallel dazu hat sich richard hordens architektur weiterentwickelt. sein antrieb ist nicht eine blinde leidenschaft für technologie, sondern vielmehr das wissen, dass technologie synergetisch wirken kann, um den menschen der natur näher zu bringen – wie er mit dem ski haus zeigt. ebenso ist er bestrebt, das gesellschaftliche zusammenleben zu verbessern, wie im falle des st mark's hospitals. diesem gedankenansatz folgend hat horden innovative und spezifische beiträge geleistet: erstmalig für die disziplin ist das postulat des technologie-transfers, ebenso die idee der microarchitecture und die einführung der aerodynamik als gestalt- und strukturformende komponente. dieser wunsch, grenzen zu überschreiten, hat nie nachgelassen, und seit 1996 stellt sich richard horden der herausforderung, wissen zu vermitteln. sein intensives engagement in der lehre zeigt sich in der qualität der arbeiten seiner studenten. hordens gedankengut gründet sich nicht auf eine ästhetik a priori, sondern auf eine akkurate und wissensreiche methodologie, dem einzigen fundamentalen wert in der architektur, welcher sich wirklich lehren und vermitteln lässt.

niccolò baldassini

in 1965 owen finlay maclaren (uk), retired aeronautical designer and former test pilot, designs the prototype baby buggy – an aluminium pushchair, which folds like an umbrella and weighs only 2.7 kg.
it is one of the most socially significant inventions of recent years.

1965 entwirft der engländer owen finlay maclaren, flugzeugdesigner im ruhestand und ehemaliger testpilot, den baby buggy-prototyp – einen aluminium kinderwagen, der sich wie ein regenschirm zusammenfalten lässt und nur 2.7 kg wiegt. er ist eine der sozial bedeutsamsten erfindungen der letzten jahre.

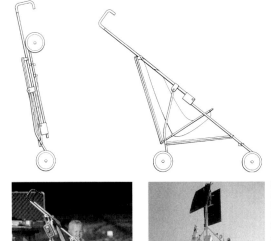

surveyor spacecraft.
like the baby buggy, it is made of aluminium and folds to fit inside the rocket nose cone.

diese mondfähre ist wie der baby buggy aus aluminium und zusammenklappbar, damit sie in die spitze der trägerrakete passt.

contents

	6	introduction
architecture	10	richard horden architect
	20	wing tower
	24	expo 2000 competition
	28	robert and lisa sainsbury wing
	32	evening hill house
	34	music room
	36	solar studio
	38	knightsbridge
	40	study gallery
	42	dulwich picture gallery
	44	artists' homes
	46	river thames monorail
	48	glass bridge
	50	poole tower
teaching	54	richard horden teacher
	58	microarchitecture
	64	beach point
	66	kayak club
	68	cliffhanger
	70	silva spider
	72	white water
	74	air camp
	76	boat house
	78	bee house
	80	weather station
	82	sky motel
	84	lakeside apartments
	86	fire station
	88	glass exhibition centre
	90	lagoon exhibition centre
	92	energy tree
	94	isar tower
	96	airship tower
	98	k1
	100	vienna fisch haus
	102	solar spider
	103	aluar – buenos aires
	104	geodetic balloons
	106	sport bridge
	108	2nd year design lectures
research	110	microgravity projects
	114	improvements to the department
institute projects	116	modular display system
	118	glass cubes project
	120	skydeck haus / smart haus
appendix	124	name index
	126	picture index
	128	acknowledgements

introduction

einführung

design is a balance of influences and objectives. it is as much an exploration of sources as the creating of particular architectural solutions: the source contains the solution as the yacht house and microarchitecture projects show. this is the case of ian mclaren's baby buggy. as an aeronautical engineer he radically changed the heavy steel framed victorian pram. his aeronautical design skills produced one of the major social innovations of the century – yet he wasn't a pram designer. burt rutan, the californian aerospace engineer, keeps himself sufficiently detached from bureaucratic aviation organisations to maintain a freedom of thinking, creating large leaps in technological innovation. his work includes realising relatively low-cost alternatives to launch space vehicles (proteus). it is these men who most inspire and drive our thoughts as architects and designers.

developing projects, we work at a new 'in between', resulting from two states of normality. 'zwischen' is

design ist ein abwägen von einflüssen und zielen. dazu gehört das erforschen von quellen der inspiration genauso wie das erarbeiten spezifischer, architektonischer lösungen – die quelle enthält oft die lösung, wie man an den yacht house und mikroarchitektur projekten sieht. dies ist auch der fall bei ian mclarens baby buggy. als luftfahrtingenieur veränderte er die alten, schweren kinderwagen radikal. mit seinen fähigkeiten aus dem flugzeugbau brachte er eine der wichtigsten sozialen innovationen des jahrhunderts hervor, ohne kinderwagendesigner zu sein. burt rutan, ein luft- und raumfahrtingenieur aus kalifornien, hält sich bewusst fern von bürokratischen luftfahrtorganisationen und erzielt immer wieder erstaunliche technologische fortschritte, wie zum beispiel ökonomische alternativen für raumtransporter (proteus). diese menschen sind es, die uns architekten stark beeinflussen. beim entwickeln unserer projekte, werden die gren-

proteus is a multipurpose aircraft for long duration high altitude operations.

proteus ist ein mehrzweckflugzeug für langzeitflüge in grosser höhe.

the german word for 'between', and we often use this to describe our innovations. the wing tower is between earth and sky, between traditional architecture and aerodynamics. the queen's stand is between marine and land architecture, and the ski haus between mountains and sky, between vernacular architecture (the traditional swiss mountain hut) and aviation (the helicopter).

'licht' and 'leicht' are the two german words for lightness and lightweight. in english we generally use only the one word 'light'. the two meanings perhaps express most clearly the prime working and teaching objectives: finding new ways to achieve more with less, optimising visual and technical lightness and developing new attitudes to minimise our indulgence in materials. a phrase we often use to encourage architects and students to think in this way: 'touch the earth lightly'.

richard horden, june 1999

zen aufgelöst und wir arbeiten in einem neuen raum der sich 'zwischen' zwei normalzuständen befindet. der wing tower befindet sich zwischen erde und himmel, zwischen traditioneller architektur und aerodynamik. queen's stand ist angesiedelt zwischen land- und schiffsarchitektur und ski haus zwischen gebirge und himmel, einheimischer architektur (die traditionelle schweizer berghütte) und der aviatik (helikopter).

das englische wort 'light' bedeutet im deutschen 'licht' und 'leicht'. beide bedeutungen drücken vielleicht am deutlichsten unsere ziele als architekten und lehrer aus: neue wege zu finden, mehr mit weniger zu erreichen, technische und visuelle leichtigkeit zu optimieren und den überfluss an materialverbrauch zu reduzieren. ein satz, den wir oft verwenden, um architekten und studenten zu ermuntern, in diese richtung zu denken, ist: 'berühre die erde sanft'.

richard horden, juni 1999

'architecture consists largely of placing something between earth and sky.'
    eero saarinen

'architektur besteht im weitesten sinne daraus, etwas zwischen himmel und erde zu plazieren.'
    eero saarinen

architecture

richard horden, architect

it was on the occasion of my 32nd birthday, when we were in the atlantic bar near the london office, that richard horden said: 'i'm more afraid of the past than the future.' his dedication to modern life, innovation and internationality drives his design work like a fresh breeze powers a sailing boat. born on the south coast of england in an internationally minded family, he grew up with sailing boats, wind, light, mobility, nature, lifestyle and spirit – elements which can all be found in his architecture. to understand richard horden's architecture, it is important to know about his origins from the south coast, with its rich sailing and high-technology environment. the fascination of the beauty and technology of a modern sailing boat informs many of his designs. his

'ich fürchte mich mehr vor der vergangenheit als vor der zukunft', sagte richard horden, als wir anlässlich meines 32. geburtstags in der atlantic bar nahe des londoner büros über die antiquierten ansichten von prinz charles bezüglich architektur diskutierten. richard hordens verpflichtung gegenüber der moderne, innovation und internationalität treibt seine arbeit als architekt an wie eine frische brise ein segelboot. geboren an der südküste von england, wuchs er in einer international denkenden familie auf. dieses umfeld von segelbooten, wind, licht, mobilität, lebensstil und -gefühl prägt seine architektur. um diese architektur zu verstehen, ist es wichtig, seine herkunft von der südenglischen küste mit ihrem grossartigen segel- und technologieumfeld zu

modern architecture
irene and peter horden in front of their new modern house in poole, built in 1972

irene and peter horden im garten ihres neuen modernen hauses in poole, gebaut 1972

modern yachts – tornado catamaran

first house, which he built for his parents, is an uncompromising modern steel-frame building, inspired by the work of californian architect craig ellwood and by the flow of spaces, nature and movement.

like design, sailing combines good intuition and fast reactions. richard horden, himself an enthusiastic yachtsman, is very quick at sketching a new idea and thus communicating it to his office, a client or students. a new project seems to be born within minutes of a sketch. even if a project takes many years to be completed, it is this first sketch, or the first model, which communicates the design idea and keeps it fresh through all the 'changing weather' of client meetings, contractor meetings and cost reduction processes. richard

kennen. die faszination, die von der schönheit und technologie moderner segelboote ausgeht, beeinflusst viele seiner entwürfe. sein erstes haus, das er für seine eltern baute, ist ein kompromisslos modernes stahlhaus, das durch die arbeiten des kalifornischen architekten craig ellwood beeinflusst und von raumfluss, natur und bewegung geprägt ist.

wie das segeln verbindet das entwerfen intuition und schnelle reaktion. richard horden, selbst passionierter segler, ist sehr schnell und geschickt im aufzeichnen einer neuen idee, um diese an sein büro, einen bauherrn oder studenten mitzuteilen und den entwurfsprozess in gang zu setzen. eine neues projekt scheint oft innerhalb von minuten mit einer neuen skizze zu entstehen. segeln erfordert

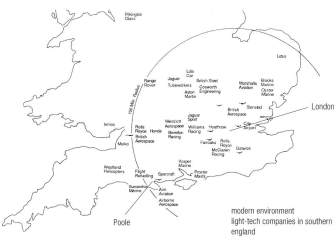

modern environment
light-tech companies in southern england

modern lifestyle
the yacht house

horden's skills in reacting fast and in a qualitative way to changes in design derive from a very positive and pro-active attitude to life.

richard horden's contribution to architecture at the turn of the millennium is to remove weight from buildings. at a time when all the items we use, like mobile phones, computers and cameras, are becoming smaller and lighter, architecture also develops in this direction. this reveals itself in his microarchitecture, which may actually be anything from lightweight mobile constructions up to big buildings like the german pavilion, which is a light, transparent structure without visual weight, symbolising a modern open and democratic society.

having trained at the aa and worked with sir norman foster and partners, he started his own office in 1984 with the yacht house series, a modular house system based on the technology of a tornado catamaran.

die fähigkeit, schnell auf sich ändernde windverhältnisse zu reagieren; eine fähigkeit, welche auch dem designer zugute kommt.

richard hordens beitrag zur architektur der jahrtausendwende ist es, den gebäuden das gewicht zu nehmen. in einer zeit, in der unsere alltagsgegenstände wie mobiltelefone, computer, kameras kleiner und leichter werden, bewegt sich auch seine architektur in diese richtung. dies zeigt sich in der vielfalt seiner projekte, angefangen bei der mikro architektur, mobile leichtbauten, bis zu grossen projekten wie dem deutschen pavillon, der mit seinem leichten und transparenten baukörper kein visuelles gewicht mehr hat und eine moderne, offene und demokratische gesellschaft repräsentiert.

nach seiner ausbildung an der aa und seiner arbeit bei sir norman foster und partner eröffnete er 1984 mit den yacht house projekten, einem

modern vehicles – airbus

modern sculpture – kenneth snelson

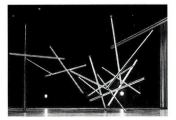

the yacht house is a series of modular houses using yacht technology.

die yacht houses sind eine serie modularer häuser, die yachtbautechnologien anwenden.

the house was built with proctor masts, a company specialising in aluminium and carbon-fibre yacht mast construction. similarly, many designs had their origins in the skill and speed of trevor green at formula spars in building aluminium prototypes. aluminium plays an important role in horden's architecture. it allows fast prototyping as well as the production of precise surfaces and shapes which reflect light in an elegant way. this applies to projects like the skihaus as well as the rooftop architecture of the robert and lisa sainsbury wing of st mark's hospital.

the care for detail put into a design is also visible in large scale buildings like the famous 'queen's stand', the club house for the royal family at the epsom derby. queen's stand is a lookout architecture informed by the elegance of modern yachts. the project for 'sydney east circular quay' reacts uniquely to the

modularen hausbausystem auf der grundlage der technologie eines tornado katamarans, sein eigenes büro. das haus wurde mit proctor masts gebaut, eine firma, die sich auf den bau von segelmasten aus aluminium und kohlefaser spezialisiert hat. auf ähnliche weise wurden viele entwürfe erst möglich durch das geschick und die geschwindigkeit von trevor green von formula spars im prototypenbau. aluminium spielt eine wichtige rolle in hordens architektur. einerseits erlaubt es, schnell prototypen zu fertigen, andererseits bietet es präzise und formbare oberflächen, die das licht auf elegante art reflektieren. dies trifft auf projekte wie das skihaus, aber auch den dachaufbau des robert and lisa sainsbury wing beim st mark's hospital zu.

die sorgfalt, die dem detail gewidmet wird, ist auch in grösseren projekten wie dem berühmten 'queen's stand' erkennbar. dieses

yacht house series yh1, built 1984

great architecture of the famous opera house and the yacht environment of sydney. while an australian firm won the competition, richard horden was contacted many years later by the institute of australian architects to present his scheme again. this happened while people were demonstrating to stop the construction of the chosen design when it became clear how a mistaken architectural concept could spoil views and the context of the opera house. for richard horden, this is the proof that good design endures and a designer always has to strive for the highest quality.

clubhaus für die königliche familie beim epsom derby pferderennplatz ist eine ausblick-architektur, die von der eleganz moderner motorjachten inspiriert ist. das projekt für den 'sydney east circular quay' reagiert auf einzigartige weise auf die architektur des berühmten opernhauses und das segelumfeld von sydney. obwohl ein australisches büro den wettbewerb gewann, wurde richard horden mehrere jahre später vom institut australischer architekten eingeladen, seinen entwurf nochmals zu präsentieren. dies geschah, während die bewohner sydneys auf die strasse gingen, um den weiterbau des siegerprojektes zu

queen's stand, 1993
a lookout architecture, informed by modern yachts

*queen's stand, 1993
eine ausblick-architektur,
inspiriert durch moderne
yachten*

left: the skihaus, 1992,
finds its place between
earth and sky.

*links: das skihaus, 1992
findet seinen ort zwischen
himmel und erde.*

while the office is working on various projects which range from door handles and furniture to large-scale projects like the wing tower, hospitals, galleries, traffic systems and bridges, richard horden is always in search of innovation and lightness. each project is a sensitive investigation of landscaping, space, light, new technologies, fun and function. he is fascinated by the technical innovation and the aesthetics of modern vehicles, which are the product of function and use, lightweight construction, new materials, good visibility, and aerodynamics. on his desk, one rarely sees architectural magazines, but magazines like 'boat international', 'pilot', 'bmw magazine', etc. his lateral thinking leads to technology transfers and thus interdisciplinary collaboration with high-synergy effects. the london office displays three model sailing boats in the window, symbolising the beauty of modern engineering and the freedom of innovative and creative thinking in architecture.

stoppen, als sichtbar wurde, wie ein falsches architektonisches konzept die sichtlinien und den kontext des opernhauses zerstören. für richard horden ist dies der beweis, dass gutes design dauerhaft ist, und der architekt und designer immer beste qualität anstreben muss.

das büro arbeitet an einer reihe von projekten, die von türgriffen und möbeln bis hin zu gebäuden wie dem wing tower, krankenhäusern, museen, verkehrssystemen und brücken die ganze spannweite des architektonischen entwerfens umfassen. gleichzeitig kümmert sich richard horden darum, der innovation und seiner forderung nach leichtigkeit in der architektur vorschub zu leisten. mit jedem projekt ist eine sorgfältige untersuchung von landschaft, raum, licht, neuen technologien, lebensstil und funktion verbunden. er ist fasziniert von der technischen innovation moderner fahrzeuge, ihrem lifestyle und ihrer ästhetischen erscheinung. ihre form

this page:
door handles and furniture designs show the range of richard horden's designs alongside architecture.

*diese seite:
türgriffe und möbelentwürfe zeigen die spannweite von richard hordens entwürfen neben der architektur.*

in an age when people do not have time for visions of the future, richard horden has a clear one: 'think light!' this sentence brings a whole new series of concepts into design and architecture: aerodynamics, motion, transparency, reduction of materials and energy. lightness also implies a more playful way of exploring new concepts to improve the environment we live in. design is a form of pro-active thinking: how people interact with their environment in a better way. this applies not only to planning and architecture, but also to economics, social relations, friendships. the future does not just happen. it is this creative design-orientated way of thinking which develops our future. seeing only the technological aspect of richard horden's work would mean not to understand its real impact. for him, architecture is the union of human beings and nature with the use of technology, not its separation. this 'in-between' state is researched through his micro-

entsteht aus funktion und gebrauch, leichtbauweise, neuen materialien, guten sichtverhältnissen, aerodynamik und ästhetik. seine fähigkeit, lateral zu denken, erzeugt immer neue technologie-transfers und damit interdisziplinäre zusammenarbeit mit hohem synergieeffekt. im schaufenster des londoner büros stehen drei modelle von rennsegelbooten, die für die schönheit der modernen ingenieurbaukunst und die freiheit eines kreativen und innovativen denkens in der architektur stehen.

in einer zeit, in der die menschen anscheinend keine zeit für visionen haben, hat richard horden eine sehr klare: 'think light!'. diese forderung bringt eine reihe ganz neuer konzepte in der architektur mit sich: aerodynamik, bewegung, transparenz, material- und energiereduktion. leichtigkeit bedeutet aber auch, auf spielerische weise neue konzepte zu entwickeln, die die lebensqualität unserer umwelt verbessern. design ist eine art von pro-aktivem denken dar-

opposite page:
sketch and watercolour of the east circular quay project in sydney show the continuity in design from the first sketch to the final presentation.

*gegenüber:
skizze und aquarell des east circular quay projektes in sydney zeigen die entwurfskontinuität von der ersten skizze bis zur präsentation des projektes.*

architecture studies like the skihaus, point lookout and the multitude of student projects designed under his guidance. to build with nature for people is one of his main objectives. the wing tower is a perfect example. usually, towers are built against gravity and windload. the wing tower, driven by the aesthetics of sculptures by brancusi and of aircraft wings, explores the use of aerodynamics in structural engineering. it is designed to use the structure to reduce the windload by turning the whole tower into the wind, which makes it appear completely weightless. the movement of the tower is controlled by the wind. to build with the forces of nature, not against them, is one of the key issues of future architecture and reflects a new understanding of nature and the ecosystem of our blue planet.

richard horden's personal environment is closely intergrated with the design process. 'the office' is always part of the family and vice versa. wherever he is, he creates a personal

über, wie menschen den austausch mit ihrer umgebung verbessern können. dies trifft nicht nur auf städtebau und architektur zu, sondern auch auf die wirtschaft, soziales zusammenleben und freundschaft. die zukunft geschieht nicht einfach, sie entsteht in unseren köpfen durch ein designorientiertes, kreatives denken. nur den technologischen aspekt von richard hordens arbeit zu betrachten, würde ihr in keiner weise gerecht. für ihn ist die architektur die verbindung von mensch und natur durch die technik, nicht ihre trennung. dieses 'dazwischen' untersucht er mit seinen microarchitecture studies, wie dem skihaus und point lookout, aber auch der vielzahl der studentenprojekte, die unter seiner anleitung entstehen. mit der natur für menschen zu bauen, ist eines seiner hauptziele. der wing tower ist dafür ein perfektes beispiel. türme wurden bisher gegen die schwerkraft und gegen den winddruck gebaut. der wing tower, inspiriert durch skulpturen

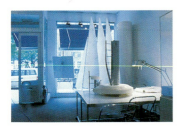

the london office with its three model yachts
das londoner büro mit den drei modellsegelbooten

modern environment, whether in the london office, his house in the new forest or at the institute in the university in munich. his wife, kathy, contributed a lot to this warm and welcoming atmosphere. her sudden death was a shock for all of us. their children, poppy and christian, continue to keep the office lively on their occasional visits.

this personal professionalism, as well as the enthusiasm of the whole design team, is a characteristic of the work of the office and therefore the architecture. design and architecture are made by people for people, just like the future.

andreas vogler, june 1999

von brancusi und der ästhetik einer tragfläche, erforscht die nutzung der aerodynamik für tragwerke. die tragstruktur wird dazu genutzt, die windlast zu reduzieren, indem der ganze turm in den wind gedreht wird, was ihn schwerelos erscheinen lässt. die bewegung des turmes wird in abhängigkeit von der windrichtung gesteuert. mit den kräften der natur zu bauen, nicht gegen sie, wird einer der kernpunkte der zukünftigen architektur sein und spiegelt ein neues verständnis gegenüber der natur und dem ökosystem unseres blauen planeten wider.

richard hordens persönliches umfeld ist eng mit dem designprozess verbunden. 'das büro' ist immer teil der familie und umgekehrt. wo er ist,

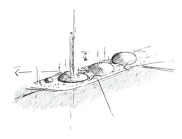

billie lee and mira esposito

sarah kirby on st mark's wing roof

mira esposito and andreas vogler in the swissair airbus a321

christian, richard, poppy and kathy horden in the finnish pavilion at venice biennale, 1997

schafft er eine persönliche, moderne atmosphäre, sei es im londoner büro, in seinem haus im new forest oder am lehrstuhl an der technischen universität in münchen. gäste aus aller welt sind herzlich willkommen. seine frau kathy trug viel zu dieser warmherzigen, offenen atmosphäre bei. ihr plötzlicher tod war ein schock für uns alle. die kinder poppy und christian halten das büro bei besuchen weiterhin auf trab.

diese persönliche professionalität wie auch der enthusiasmus aller beteiligten charakterisiert die arbeit des büros und damit die architektur. design und architektur wird von menschen für menschen gemacht, genauso wie die zukunft.

andreas vogler, juni 1999

the wing tower in glasgow
der wing tower in glasgow

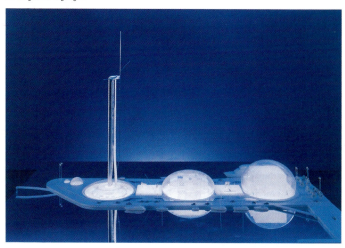

wing tower

project: london 1993
location: glasgow
design team: sarah forbes waller
richard horden
sarah kirby
billie lee
andreas vogler
engineering: peter heppel, buro happold
costs: davis langdon & everest
models: amalgam

this project was the winning design for an international competition for a 'tower for glasgow' in 1993. in 1999 the tower is under construction for completion in 2001.

the 140-m-high design is intended to inspire young people in glasgow into a future of light and digital engineering. the technical design concept is aerodynamic and the tower is rotated into wind to reduce aerodynamic drag whilst minimising weight and structural costs.

the control servos are operated automatically by computers fed with information from the atlantic weather system satellites, aviation and marine

mit diesem projekt gewannen wir 1993 den ersten preis des internationalen wettbewerbs 'a tower for glasgow'. 1999 wurde mit den bauarbeiten begonnen, die im jahr 2001 abgeschlossen werden.

das 140 m hohe bauwerk soll ein symbol sein für eine von leichtigkeit und computertechnik geprägte zukunft. es wurde nach aerodynamischen gesichtspunkten entworfen: um den luftwiderstand zu reduzieren und dadurch gewicht und kosten für das tragwerk einzusparen, lässt sich der gesamte turm in den wind drehen. die stellmotoren werden von computern gesteuert, die von wetter-

peter heppel testing the model in the wind tunnel at bmp
peter heppel mit dem modell im windkanal bei bmp

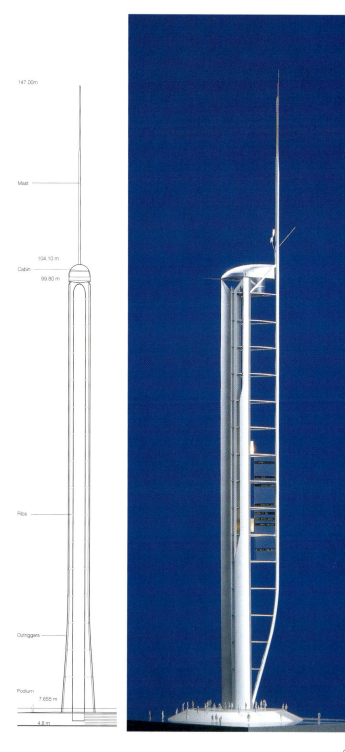

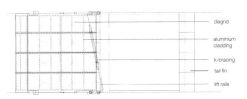
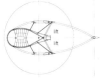

elevation of 6 m cladding section
ansicht eines 6 m hohen turmabschnitts

plan of tower
regelgrundriss turm

data. the rotating 300-ton steel structure is supported on a 70 cm spherical bearing at the base. the tower can be raised hydraulically by 25 mm for changing the components. the horizontal bearings are also interchangeable. the two rack-and-pinion lifts have individual car mounted motors for safety and can be lowered slowly to ground level without power.

visitors will enter the lifts at concourse level inside the podium and have panoramic views of the city and the river clyde from the viewing cabin at 100 m altitude. the competition design concept was developed with peter heppel, a highly experienced aeronautical engineer.

satelliten die gleichen daten erhalten wie die luft- und seefahrt.

der 300 tonnen schwere stahlturm dreht sich auf einem 70 cm starken kugellager in seinem fundament. er kann hydraulisch um 25 mm angehoben werden, um teile des lagers auszuwechseln. die horizontalen lager sind ebenfalls auswechselbar. es gibt zwei zahnrad-getriebene aufzüge, die eigene motoren auf der kabine haben, um auch bei stromausfall langsam ins erdgeschoss hinab fahren zu können.

besucher betreten die aufzüge ebenerdig im turmsockel. von der aussichtskabine in 100 m höhe geniessen sie einen herrlichen rundumblick über glasgow und den clyde. der wettbewerbsentwurf wurde zusammen mit peter heppel, einem sehr erfahrenen luftfahrtingenieur entwickelt.

richard horden discussing details on the wing tower model with mike cook.

richard horden und mike cook besprechen details am wing-tower-modell.

section through base
schnitt durch die basis

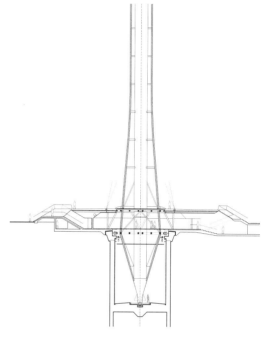

check-in / exhibition level plan
grundriss eingangs- und ausstellungsebene

38 m

Exhibition
Toilets
Plant
Exit
Entry
Plant
Check - In
Reception
Exhibition

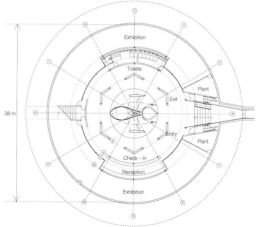

base: model and sketch
sockel: modell und skizze

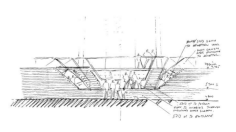

expo 2000 competition

project:	munich 1997	structural engineer:	sailer, stepan und partner ingenieure, munich
location:	hannover		
client:	trägergesellschaft deutscher pavillon mbH	mechanics and electrics:	hl-technik, munich
design team:	gerhard abel	daylight:	bartenbach lichtlabor gmbh
	christian ferber	landscaping:	büro realgrün, munich
	lydia haack	models:	frieder grüne
	richard horden		leslie stein
	birgitta kunsch	area:	16,000 m²
	billie lee	year:	1997
	eva neumeyer		
	claudia pöppel		
	jan schabert		
	leslie stein		
	thomas straub		
	craig synnestvedt		
	andreas vogler		

the design won second prize in the international competition for the german pavilion.

as the first major pavilion at the main entrance, it is a transparent visible architecture informed by the simple analogy to a tree which shelters from rain, filters light and gains energy from it. based on a 100 m radius, the curved glass roof shell contains a fine grain of photovoltaic cells laminated between glass. these are used to pump water from the small reflecting pool touching the south edge of the roof, forming a continuous rippling cascade of water keeping the roof cool. a system of computer-controlled louvres creates an 'active' roof, which can adjust to specific lighting demands inside. further, it can create changing light situations with daylight and artificial light at night. the possible dramatic sets of light would make the building a great contribution to exhibition architecture.

the simple linear structure of inclined columns allows office buildings

der entwurf gewann den zweiten preis im internationalen wettbewerb für den deutschen pavillon.

die transparente architektur dieses ersten grossen pavillons am haupteingang leitet sich von der analogie eines baumes ab, der vor regen schützt, licht filtert und daraus energie gewinnt. das gebogene glasdach beschreibt einen radius von 100 m und enthält zwischen den scheiben eine filigrane struktur aus photozellen. mit dem erzeugten strom wird wasser zur kühlung der dachhaut aus dem auf der südseite gelegenen wasserbecken zum dachfirst gepumpt. computergesteuerte sonnenblenden reagieren auf unterschiedliche lichtbedürfnisse im innenraum. es entsteht ein 'aktives' dach, das mit tages- und kunstlicht verschiedene stimmungen erzeugen kann. mit seinen spektakulären lichtinszenierungen wäre das gebäude ein wichtiger beitrag zur ausstellungsarchitektur.

die geneigten stützen werden von der verspannten konstruktion

like a tree, the roof filters light and gains energy from it.

das dach funktioniert wie ein baum, der das licht filtert und dabei energie gewinnt.

the curved roof shape opens towards the expo plaza.

die runde dachform öffnet sich zum expo-plaza hin.

the roof concept derives from the umbrella leaning into wind open on the leeward side.

die dachform leitet sich von einem regenschirm ab, der gegen den wind gelehnt wird und nach lee hin offen ist.

aerial view from east
aufsicht von osten

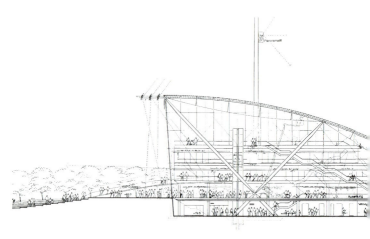

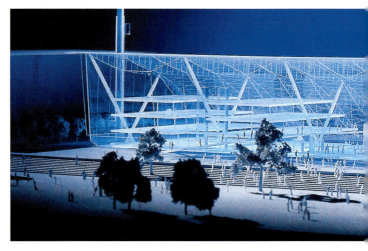

to be inserted after expo and is braced by the cable diagrid roof support system. the roof concept derives from the umbrella leaning into wind open on the leaward side. the structural concept aimed to produce an extremely light glass-steel assembly in the tradition of the glass houses of kew gardens. as the main entrance pavilion, the project symbolizes germany as an open, innovative and future-orientated society.

des daches gehalten. sie stehen in einem abstand, der gross genug ist, um nach der expo büroflächen dazwischen einzufügen. dieses tragwerkskonzept führt zu einer besonders leichten stahl-glas-konstruktion in tradition der gewächshäuser von kew gardens. mit diesem projekt soll sich deutschland als eine offene, innovative und zukunftsorientierte gesellschaft präsentieren.

cross-section
querschnitt

a 'media bridge' is leading through the volume of the pavilion, which allows experiencing space and information.

eine 'medienbrücke' führt durch das volumen und macht raum und information vielfältig erlebbar.

the robert and lisa sainsbury wing
st mark's hospital

project:	england 1994-95
location:	northwick park, london
design team:	sarah forbes-waller
	kathy horden
	richard horden
	sarah kirby
	billie lee
	sarah north
engineering:	withby and bird
costs:	davis, langdon and everest
lighting:	george sexton associates
services:	loren butt & yates associates
models:	amalgam

robert and lisa sainsbury have been consistently generous, understanding and sympathetic clients. the specialist care clinic was donated to james thomson, surgeon and director of st mark's hospital. lisa sainsbury had been a nurse and enjoyed discussing the project with kathy, my wife, who was a nurse as well. she was to be a wonderful help in ensuring that a strong sense of 'care' was visible in the design. this was done particularly effectively with

robert und lisa sainsbury waren über jahre hinweg grosszügige und verständnisvolle bauherren. so ist die fachärztliche pflegeklinik eine spende an den chirurg und chefarzt am st. mark's hospital, james thomson. lisa sainsbury ist ausgebildete krankenschwester. sie genoss es, mit meiner frau kathy, ebenfalls krankenschwester, über das projekt zu diskutieren. es ist kathy zu verdanken, dass der entwurf ein gefühl der geborgenheit und fürsorge ausstrahlt.

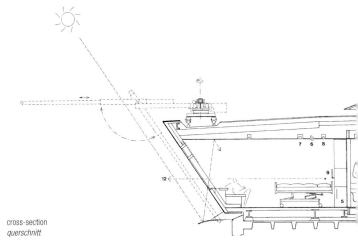

cross-section
querschnitt

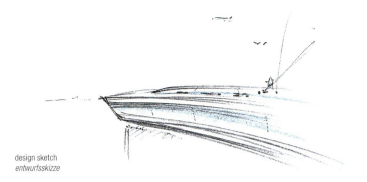

design sketch
entwurfsskizze

aluminium boat
aluminiumboot

roof cowl
dachhaube

the sloping glass allows clear views.
die geneigte verglasung ermöglicht eine klare sicht.

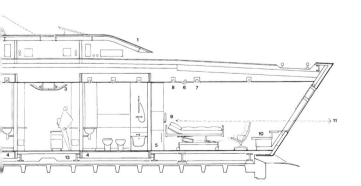

1. external glass lift	1. verglaster aussenlift
2. reception	2. empfang
3. consulting rooms	3. behandlungszimmer
4. high-dependency unit	4. überwachungsstation
5. day room	5. aufenthaltszimmer
6. nurses' station	6. krankenstation
7. internal lifts	7. innenliegende aufzüge

the gentle indirect lighting design informed by the airbus interior, with washington gallery lighting designer george sexton, also a close friend of the sainsbury's. the close attention to colour and detail is symbolised by the lightest white crockery kathy could find from crossair and british airways. light crockery and cutlery being an important factor for patients in care.

eine wichtige rolle spielt die sanfte indirekte beleuchtung, die zusammen mit george sexton, lichtdesigner der washington gallery und ebenfalls ein guter freund der sainsburys, entwickelt wurde.

ein beispiel für die bedeutung von details und farben in der ausstattung ist das weisse geschirr von crossair und british airways – das leichteste, das kathy finden konnte. denn leichtes geschirr und besteck ist sehr wichtig für pflegepatienten.

the fully glazed elevator allows a direct access of the rooftop extension on the 9-storey northwick park hospital.

der voll verglaste aufzug erlaubt einen direkten zugang zu der erweiterung auf dem dach des 9-geschossigen northwick park krankenhauses.

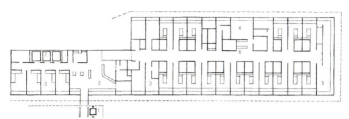

floorplan - grundriss

ceiling design and indirect lighting of the airbus interior informed the design of the aisle.

die deckengestaltung und das indirekte licht im airbus war vorbild für die beleuchtung des flurs.

the reception of the hospital is conceived as a 'check-in' desk, where patients get their information brochures and are cared for from the minute of their arrival.

die rezeption des krankenhauses ist wie ein 'check-in', wo die patienten ihre informationsbroschüren erhalten und vom ersten moment an umsorgt werden.

evening hill house
poole

project:	london 1996
location:	evening hill, poole
design team:	mira esposito
	richard horden
	sarah kirby
engineering:	tony hunt
costs:	denley king partnership
models:	modelogic

'evening hill' is the name given to one of the finest viewpoints in southern england. the panorama extends from the isle of wight, the english channel to the chalk cliffs of the purbeck hills with a foreground of the rich activity of sailboard, yacht racing, yacht clubs and cross channel ferries. brownsea island, a nature reserve is in the centre of the view over poole harbour. the poole bay has a special microclimate and the house is designed to optimise this southern aspect. the curving, seagull wing-like roof form completes the shape and makes the house appear to fly low over the gently sloping hillside.

'evening hill' ist die bezeichnung für einen der schönsten aussichtspunkte südenglands. das panorama reicht von der isle of wight über den kanal bis zu den kreidefelsen der purbeck hills. im vordergrund ein geschäftiges treiben von segelbooten, regatten, yachtklubs und kanalfähren. im zentrum des blicks über den hafen von poole liegt das naturschutzgebiet brownsea island. in der bucht von poole herrscht ein südliches mikroklima, das vom haus genutzt wird. das geschwungene, einem möwenflügel nachempfundene dach vollendet die form, das haus scheint über den leichten abhang zu gleiten.

south elevation
südfassade

White Painted Steel or Alu

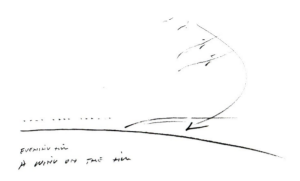

evening sun
A wind on the hill

view from the south (above)
and from north (right)

*blick von süden (oben) und
von norden (rechts)*

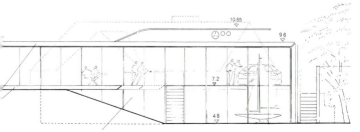

Aluminum Frame with Triple Glazed Window

music room
bryanston

project:	london 1998
location:	bryanston, dorset
design team:	richard horden
	birgitta kunsch
	billie lee
client:	bryanston school
engineering:	wsp
costs:	denley king partnership
models:	rha

this tiny 'human scale' project is one of my favourites. the charming english family sanchez, david and daughter poppy simpson, sponsored the music room for a girl's house within the school. the project design is most significant for the way the building is recessed into the chalk hillside looking out onto its own sheltered courtyard. in dorset the wind blows very strongly from the west, so the small excavated external space is warm and welcoming in an otherwise bleak landscape. the roof beams and courtyard wall extend into and over the landscape. the roof appears to float over the grassy landscape creating a 'zwischen' zone between building, earth and sky.

dieser kleine anbau ist eines meiner lieblingsprojekte. die reizende englische familie sanchez, david und tochter poppy simpson, stiftete das musikzimmer für ein mädchenwohnheim der schule. charakteristisch für den entwurf ist die art und weise, wie das gebäude in den kreideabhang abgesenkt ist und dabei in seinen eigenen, geschützten hof blickt. in dorset weht ein starker wind aus westen und so wirkt dieser kleine, tiefer gelegene aussenraum warm und einladend in einer sonst rauhen landschaft. die dachträger und die wand zum hof erstrecken sich in die landschaft. das dach scheint über der wiese zu schweben und bildet so eine eigene zone zwischen gebäude, erde und himmel.

the sheltered courtyard looking south

blick nach süden in den geschützten hof

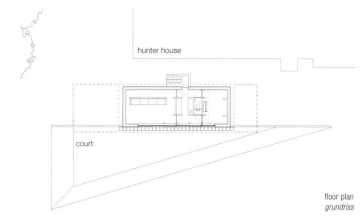

floor plan
grundriss

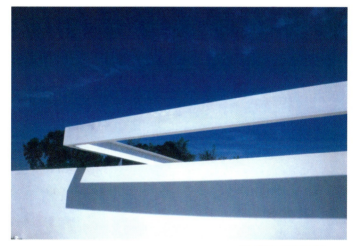

the roof beamer appears to float above and embrace the surrounding landscape.

der dachträger scheint über der landschaft zu schweben und sie zu umarmen.

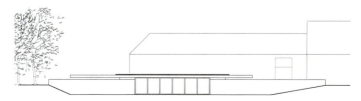

section through courtyard towards hunter house
schnitt durch den hof mit blick aufs hunter house

solar studio
hampstead

project:	london 1996
location:	hampstead
design team:	richard horden
	sabine kaufmann
costs:	120.000 gbp
energy:	mark crawford, bp solar
models:	sabine kaufmann
client:	sheila coope-jalving

the individual and multiple solar cells produce energy and form shading similar to the leaves of a tree.

einzelne und kombinierte solarzellen erzeugen energie und spenden schatten, ähnlich wie die blätter eines baumes.

transparency and shading – the characteristics of a tree in leaf

transparenz und verschattung – die eigenschaften eines belaubten baumes

designed for a friend of the family sheila coope-jalving, this small one-bedroom studio house was designed with zurich eth student sabine kaufmann and mark crawford from bp solar. the flat roof and south-facing shutters contain photovoltaic cells collecting energy from london's often overcast or shaded sky. assuming house owners are at work during the day, leaving primary electrical power for refrigerator and control circuits only, the cells provide extra energy during the day which is fed into the national grid. the concept of solar cell and leaf, house and tree was informed by susannah hagan's lecture at the solar conference in berlin 1996.

dieses kleine zweizimmerhaus für eine freundin der familie, sheila coope-jalving, wurde zusammen mit einer studentin der eth zürich, sabine kaufmann, und mark cornford von bp solar entworfen. flachdach und südfassade sind mit solarzellen bestückt, die auch aus londons oft bedecktem oder schattigem himmel strom gewinnen. wenn die bewohner tagsüber arbeiten, und kühlschrank und steuerungstechnik die einzigen energieverbraucher sind, kann der überschüssige strom gegen eine vergütung der stromgesellschaft in das öffentliche netz eingespeist werden. die analogie von solarzelle und blatt, haus und baum wurde durch susannah hagans vortrag auf der berliner solarkonferenz 1996 angeregt.

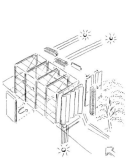

the house is designed as a 'kit' to be site assembled. the brick outer skin is added later.

das haus ist als bausatz entworfen, der vor ort zusammengebaut wird. die aussenhaut aus ziegel wird später hinzugefügt.

the leaf and the tree have similar structure and form.

blatt und baum ähneln sich in aufbau und form.

study model
arbeitsmodell

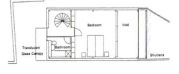

first-floor plan
erstes geschoss

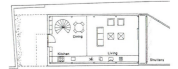

ground-floor plan
erdgeschossgrundriss

knightsbridge

project: london 1999
location: london
design team: stephen cherry
richard horden
engineering: wsp
costs: gardiner and theobald
services: j. roger preston
size: 100.000 m²
models: unit 22

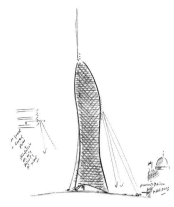

this large site owned by the prudential insurance company is located opposite harrods in london's fashionable knightsbridge district. the earlier team of canadian architects had proposed a banal red brick design which was rejected by westminster city planning department and the royal fine arts commission. my task, together with stephen cherry, was to restructure the design and achieve a fast-track planning permission. this was achieved in three months. a full site masterplan, using the economist plaza by alison and peter smithson as a reference, was also formulated. it included a 30-floor tower containing offices, apartments, shops and a health centre. the design was enthusiastically welcomed by westminster head of planning alan bradley. my proposal was that the development should be called the 'princess diana centre', with its proximity to harrods and midway between princess diana's house at kensington palace and buckingham palace.

dieses grosse grundstück der prudential insurance company liegt gegenüber harrods, dem bekannten kaufhaus in londons elegantem stadtteil knightsbridge. zunächst wurde ein kanadisches architektenteam beauftragt, deren entwurf ein banales gebäude aus rotem ziegel vorsah. dies wurde vom westminster city planning department und der royal fine arts commission abgelehnt. meine aufgabe war, den entwurf zusammen mit stephen cherry zu überarbeiten, um schnellstmöglich eine planungsgenehmigung zu erhalten. binnen drei monaten wurde das ziel erreicht und ein bebauungsplan mit 30-stöckigem wohn-, geschäfts-, und bürohochhaus nach dem vorbild des economist plaza von alison und peter smithson erstellt.

aufgrund der nähe des neuen gebäudekomplexes zu harrods und der lage des grundstücks zwischen buckingham- und kensington palace war mein vorschlag, das projekt 'princess diana centre' zu nennen.

the study model shows the tower orientation towards harrods and buckingham palace.

die modellstudie zeigt die orientierung des turms richtung harrods und buckingham palace.

harrods

brompton road

knightsbridge

study gallery
poole

project:	london 1994
location:	poole, dorset
design team:	mira esposito
	richard horden
	ben knight
	billie lee
	tom roberts
	jeremy main
	raj suresh narputharaj
supporters:	millennium commission
	henry moore foundation
	local individuals and
	organisations
costs:	denley king and partners
models:	amalgam

the study gallery and sculpture court is primarily designed to inspire children into exploring modern art and sculpture. the carefully scaled design acknowledges that most visitors will be less than 1.5 m tall! children will be encouraged to design and build light sculpture to be illuminated and exhibited in the 12-m-high display space, visible from the centre of poole.

the study gallery, as its name implies, has two functions: firstly, to display the collection of poole college, the owner of the land, and secondly, to be the focus for teaching in the region of dorset, guided by curator jeremy main. thanks to the patience and determination of tom roberts, over five years the project received the financial backing of the millennium commission, henry moore foundation and many local individuals and organisations. the college collection included work by henry moore, elisabeth frink and barbara hepworth, and anthony caro is a member of the gallery trust.

die study gallery mit ihrem skulpturenhof soll kinder dazu anregen, sich mit moderner kunst, insbesondere skulpturen auseinanderzusetzen. der entwurf berücksichtigt in seiner masstäblichkeit, dass der grossteil der besucher kleiner als 1.50 m sein wird! die kinder können einfache skulpturen entwerfen und bauen, die im 12 m hohen galerieraum ausgestellt werden, gut sichtbar von pooles stadtmitte.

wie der name andeutet, hat die study gallery unter der leitung von jeremy main zwei aufgaben: erstens die sammlung des poole college auszustellen, zu der werke von henry moore, elisabeth frink und barbara hepworth zählen, und zweitens mittelpunkt der kunstausbildung in der region dorsets zu sein.

dank der geduld und entschlossenheit von tom roberts hat das projekt nach fünf jahren die finanzielle unterstützung von zahlreichen organisationen und privatleuten erhalten.

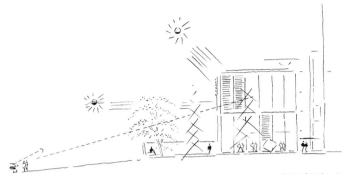

sketch of the facade
fassadenstudie

the sculpture court extends the volume of the ground floor space.

der skulpturenhof erweitert den erdgeschossraum.

changing facades
wechselndes erscheinungsbild

site plan with sculpture garden
lageplan mit skulpturengarten

dulwich picture gallery
london

project:	london 1992
location:	dulwich
design team:	mira esposito
	richard horden
	brian kelly
	sarah kirby
	sarah north
clients:	dulwich picture gallery
	sir robert and lady sainsbury
lighting:	george sexton associates
services:	loren butt and cowther and co.
history:	paula deitz
models:	amalgam

the dulwich picture gallery was designed by john soane in 1817 and was the first purpose-built art gallery in england. sir robert and lisa sainsbury financed this proposal to provide the gallery with proper storage and maintenance facilities below the existing building. a new public entrance and teaching facilities are located to the south, a secure loading zone at the north end. the whole project is designed to optimise the view of the beautiful garden, create a sheltered sculpture courtyard and a south orientated 'energy roof' with glass integrated photovoltaics.

die dulwich picture gallery wurde 1817 von john soane entworfen, es war der erste museumsneubau in england. robert und lisa sainsbury finanzierten die vorschläge für eine erweiterung des museums. der entwurf sieht vor, dass der wunderbare park erhalten wird und ein geschützter skulpturengarten neu entsteht. dem altbau wird im süden ein neuer, lichter eingangspavillon mit seminarräumen und einem photovoltatischen glasdach angefügt, im norden eine geschützte anlieferung. unter dem altbau entstehen zusätzliche depots und werkstätten.

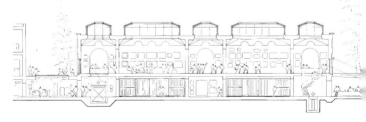

curator's office and translucent
glass art handling spaces

*büro des kurators und verglaste
anlieferungs- und unterhaltsräume*

the dulwich picture gallery with
storage areas below

*die gemäldegalerie in dulwich
mit depots im untergeschoss*

section - *schnitt*

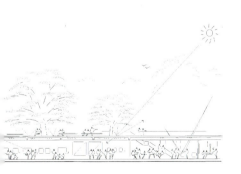

sunken, glass-roofed entrance building maintains existing garden

der tieferliegende, glasgedeckte eingang bewahrt den garten

model view of the proposed gallery extension

modellansicht der vorgeschlagenen museumserweiterung

artists' homes
dorset

project: london 1992
location: bere regis, dorset
design team: richard horden
 sarah kirby
 mike wigginton
clients: cyril wood trust
engineering: tony hunt
costs: denley king partnership
models: rha

designed as a memorial to cyril wood, who founded the arts council in england, the project was financed by the cyril wood trust, which is lead by wood's wife rosalind and well known english artists, writers and musicians, including yehudi menuhin and john le carré. the project provides 26 homes for elderly artists, musicians and craftspeople, a workshop, studio and art gallery. like the courtyard house in poole, this project is best understood as a sequence of spaces from public to private: public square, gallery, private community square, studio, workshop, covered and landscaped path to private individual living spaces, and opening onto private outside terraces with views south over the dorset landscape.

the project was built for a remarkably low budget of £400/sqm.

dieses projekt entstand zum gedenken an cyril wood, den gründer des 'art council', und wurde vom 'cyril wood trust', unter der leitung von woods ehefrau rosalind und bekannten englischen künstlern wie yehudi menuhin und john le carré finanziert. das projekt umfasst 26 wohnungen für ältere künstler, musiker und kunsthandwerker, eine werkstatt, ein atelier und eine kunstgalerie. ähnlich wie das courtyard house in poole ist dieses projekt als raumabfolge vom öffentlichen zum privaten raum zu verstehen: platz, galerie, interne freifläche, atelier, werkstatt, gedeckter und landschaftlich gestalteter weg zu den privaten wohnräumen und schliesslich die öffnung auf private terrassen mit blick auf die landschaft von dorset.

das projekt wurde für einen bemerkenswert niedrigen preis von £400/qm realisiert.

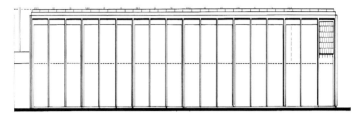

elevation
ansicht

model

covered path
gedeckter weg

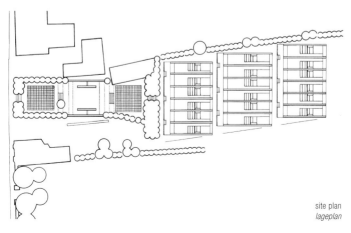

site plan
lageplan

river thames monorail

projects:	london 1995
location:	london
design team:	mira esposito
	richard horden
	sarah kirby
	andreas vogler
models:	unit 22
cost:	clyde malby
	thyssen (munich)
	bombardier (canada)
consultant:	neil steward

the river thames has a tidal range of 7 m with very strong currents. this means that the river edges are not usable at mid and low tides, and waterbuses are highly polluting because of the need for powerful diesel engines to overcome the force of the tide. this proposal for a light, fast monorail would occupy this 'zwischen' zone with a rail floating above high tide level and running beneath the southern arches of the existing bridges. marine pile construction is relatively cheap and uncomplicated by avoiding complex city land ownerships. the cost for a 5-mile section from the millennium dome to westminster would be £50m compared with £300m for an underground system. the monorail would connect heathrow to central london and the city airport, linking key london landmarks with a fast, elegant, non polluting river monorail.

the model is on exposition at the london transport museum.

der wasserstand der themse schwankt gezeitenbedingt um bis zu 7 m bei sehr starken strömungen. die ufernahen bereiche sind nur bei hohem pegelstand nutzbar, zusätzlich belasten wassertaxis die umwelt übermässig, da sie leistungsstarke dieselmotoren benötigen, um die starken strömungen zu überwinden.

dies inspirierte zum entwurf einer eleganten, umweltfreundlichen schnellbahn am südufer der themse, die auf einer schiene über dem hochwasserpegel, aber unter bestehenden brückenbögen dahingleitet. sie verbindet heathrow mit dem zentrum londons und dem city airport.

eine realisierung wäre deutlich günstiger als herkömmliche u-bahn-strecken, da pfahlkonstruktionen preiswert und unkompliziert zu verwirklichen sind und strittige eigentumsfragen umgangen werden können. ein fünf meilen langer bauabschnitt vom millennium dome bis westminster würde £50.000 kosten; eine u-bahn-strecke £300.000!

the monorail could link key london landmarks with two airports.

die einschienenbahn könnte bedeutende londoner wahrzeichen mit zwei flughäfen verbinden.

the monorail along the thames would stop at some of the major landmarks in london.

der monorail entlang der themse würde an einigen der bedeutensten sehenswürdigkeiten londons halt machen.

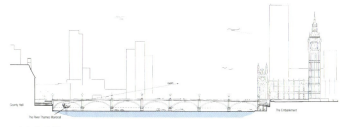

westminster bridge

glass bridge

projects:	london 1996	students:	architecture students from eth, zurich
location:	river thames, london		m+e students from hta, lucerne
design team:	mira esposito, richard horden, andreas vogler	coaching:	a. compagno, l. ilg, d. nguyen dai, m. trawnika, a. vogler
engineering:	withby and bird	client:	peabody trust
energy:	prof. klaus daniels, eth zurich		

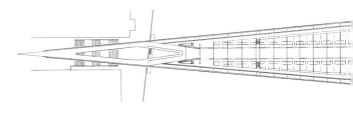

the glass bridge is a further development of the living bridge linking st paul's and the new tate gallery in london. together with klaus daniels and his students from eth zurich, the concept was extended to a full energy gaining bridge powered by wind, solar cells and tidal changes using its aerodynamic shape for natural ventilation and cooling. the two-level bridge contains shops and fully serviced apartments with a solar shuttle linking both river banks: a modern proposal referencing the old london bridge with its houses.

the over 2-m-long model was shown in london, moscow, hong kong and japan.

die 'glassbridge' ist eine weiterentwicklung des 'living bridge'-projekts, das die st. pauls kathedrale über die themse hinweg mit der neuen tate gallery verbindet. gemeinsam mit klaus daniels und seinen zürcher studenten haben wir das konzept erweitert und eine energie-autarke brücke entworfen, die aus wind, sonne und gezeiten strom gewinnt, und deren aerodynamische form die natürliche belüftung und klimatisierung unterstützt. die zweigeschossige brücke enthält läden und wohnungen; ein solarbus verbindet beide flussufer miteinander: eine moderne neuinterpretation der alten london bridge mit ihren häusern. das über 2 m lange modell wurde in london, moskau, hongkong und japan ausgestellt.

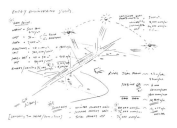

prof. klaus daniels

plan
grundriss

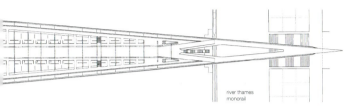

river thames
monorail

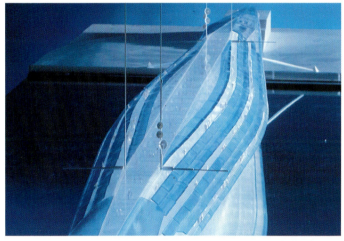

aerodynamics

light and construction

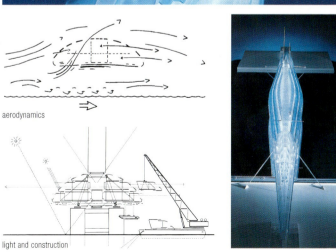

poole tower

project: london 1997
location: poole, dorset
design team: richard horden
billie lee
engineering: peter heppel
models: neil king

'bird in space', sculpture by constantin brancusi

'vogel im raum', skulptur von constantin brancusi

designed at the request of poole council as a millennium observation tower, poole tower is a relative of the earlier wing tower. the structural concept is similar to a 'fish on a stick'. the central tapering steel column is the primary structure surrounded by an aerodynamic aluminium cladding. this is supported on bearings turning in a controlled way to point into the wind. lifts would be fitted to tracks as part of the exterior surface. the shiny silver surface would be a perfectly smooth flush detailed skin, reflecting light as it turns. as with the wing tower, the form was inspired by brancusi's 'bird in space' and work by usa sculptor ellsworth kelly.

der 'millennium observation tower' wurde im auftrag des stadtrats von poole entworfen. er ist ein verwandter des frühen wing tower.

das statische konzept ähnelt dem bild eines 'steckerlfischs'. um die zentrale, spitz zulaufende stahlstütze dreht sich die aerodynamisch geformte aluminiumverkleidung kontrolliert in den wind. die aufzüge sind bestandteil der vollkommen glatten, silber glänzenden fassade, in der sich bei jeder drehung die sonne spiegelt. die formgebung des poole tower wurde wie schon der wingtower durch brancusis skulptur 'vogel im raum' und arbeiten des amerikanischen bildhauers ellsworth kelly beeinflusst.

tapering forms, *konische formen*

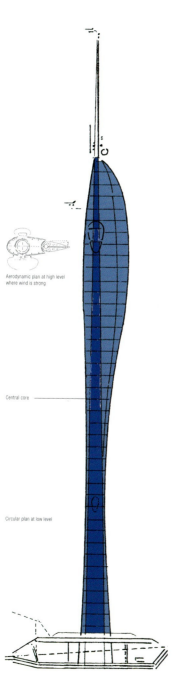

Aerodynamic plan at high level where wind is strong

Central core

Circular plan at low level

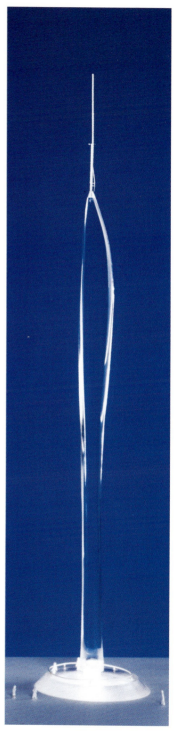

teaching

richard horden, teacher

it is a privilege to teach in munich, as it is one of the finest environments for the development of architecture and product design. munich is one of the cities of the 'alpine ring', together with centres like vienna, geneva, zurich, turin, milan, and venice. students have access to wonderfully rich cultural and urban environments, but, more significantly, access to an enormous range of beautiful geographic locations for their projects, from flat meandering rivers in the plains to the hundreds of lakes, such as starnberg and kochelsee, the wooded pre-alps, forests, fast-flowing rivers, steep gorges and valleys close to the high snowy peaks of the northern alps.

like london, it is a city of intensely busy workbenches and highly focused creativity and design. the region contains some of the finest industrial organizations in central europe: bmw, bulthaup, audi, man, siemens, with the largest pv solar installation in the world, advanced aerospace industries, dornier and eurocopter and the

in münchen zu unterrichten ist ein privileg, da die stadt ideale voraussetzungen für die ausbildung von architekten und produktdesignern bietet. die nähe zu den alpen verbindet sie mit städten wie wien, zürich, genf, turin, mailand und venedig. die studenten können wertvolle kultur- und stadtlandschaften erleben, doch wichtiger ist die enorme bandbreite an schön gelegenen standorten für ihre projekte: sanft geschwungene flussläufe in der ebene, zahlreiche seen wie der starnberger- oder kochelsee, die bewaldeten voralpen, wälder, reissende flüsse, steile schluchten und täler, nahe der schneebedeckten gipfel der nördlichen alpen.

wie london ist die stadt ein geschäftiger produktionsstandort, der von high-tech-industrie geprägt ist. viele von europas führenden firmen haben in der region ihren sitz: bmw, bulthaup, audi, man sowie siemens, die auf der messe die weltgrösste solaranlage gebaut haben. die luft- und raumfahrt ist mit dornier, eurocopter

bmw headquarters

olympic stadium

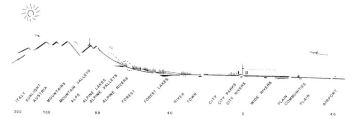

european control centre for the international space station, the ecologically focused fraunhofer institute, the finest design tradition from otl aicher and max bill at the former hochschule für gestaltung in ulm, plus one of the finest airports in europe – also with graphic design by otl aicher.

the teaching task is to optimise this rich environment for the benefit of students. the first process is simply to teach and encourage them to observe buildings and good quality environments, giving clear and contrasting examples of good and poor solutions, and explaining how to achieve quality and well-considered design. most german, austrian and swiss students have a high sense of quality and understand the benefits of fine modern design. our teaching nurtures this and adds an international awareness to enable students to move usefully into offices in london, the us, australia, etc. our interests are focused on the second half of the 20th century, especially the california

und dem europäischen kontrollzentrum der internationalen raumstation vertreten, die umweltforschung mit dem fraunhofer institut. otl aicher und max bill haben mit der hochschule für gestaltung in ulm eine grossartige designtradition begründet, in der auch das grafikdesign des münchener flughafens steht, der zu den besten in europa zählt.

an unserem lehrstuhl wollen wir den studenten diese wertvolle umgebung erschliessen. wir bringen sie dazu, gebäude und ihre umwelt zu analysieren, indem wir ihnen gute und schlechte lösungen beispielhaft vor augen führen und ihnen erklären, wie man zu guten und überlegten entwürfen kommt. die meisten studenten haben ein gutes gespür für qualität und modernes design, das wir mit unserem unterricht fördern wollen. unser hauptinteresse gilt der zweiten hälfte des 20. jahrhunderts, vor allem der kalifornischen schule mit charles und ray eames, craig ellwood und richard neutra. die arbeit und darstellungs-

map of 'alpine ring'

logo of munich airport

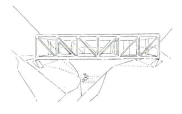

weekend house by craig ellwood
wochenendhaus von craig ellwood

school, including charles and ray eames, craig ellwood and richard neutra, and because of my past involvement with him from 1975 to 1985, a high emphasis on the design work and presentation techniques of sir norman foster.

the second phase of our teaching process involves microarchitecture – students develop fast track skills in integrating verbal and visual presentation and confidence in sketching, drawing, model building, 3d computer modelling, photography and photomontages. the designs develop using munich's rich urban, natural and alpine environment, and its high level of technical innovation and quality in product design.

many students realise their projects full size: for example beach point, air camp, cliffhanger, silva spider, fisch haus or microgravity designs and prototypes for the international space station crew quarters. here i would like to thank the young enthusiastic team of 'alu-meier', an aluminium proto-typ-

technik von sir norman foster spielt nicht zuletzt wegen meiner mitarbeit in seinem büro von 1975 bis 1985 eine grosse rolle.

in einer weiteren phase der ausbildung beschäftigen wir uns mit mikroarchitektur. dabei lernen die studenten schnell, ihre entwürfe mündlich und visuell zu präsentieren. sie gewinnen selbstvertrauen beim skizzieren, zeichnen, modellbauen, fotografieren und erstellen von fotomontagen und 3d computermodellen. beim entwerfen wird auf den landschaftlichen kontext münchens ebenso zurückgegriffen wie auf die technischen möglichkeiten und innovationen sowie den qualitätsstandard im produktdesign.

viele studenten bauen ihre entwürfe in voller grösse: beispielsweise beach point, air camp, cliffhanger, silva spider, fisch haus oder die mikrogravitationsentwürfe und prototypen für die aufenthaltsbereiche der internationalen raumstation. an dieser stelle möchte ich dem jungen und begeisterten team von 'alu-meier', ei-

beach point was produced with the help of alu-meier, munich (far left).
all components fit in three transport boxes (left).

beach point wurde mit unterstützung von alu-meier, münchen, gefertigt (links aussen).
alle komponenten können in drei transportboxen verstaut werden (links).

ing workshop in munich and other supporters of our institute.

the satisfaction as a teacher is in seeing a sea of new faces at the beginning of a semester and getting to know and help the students to realise and learn faster than they expected. some arrive at highly innovative research solutions which are then developed and marketed through industry. this would not be possible without the great support of an enthusiastic team of assistants, who dedicate of lot of their time to teaching and research parallel to realizing their own projects as architects.

richard horden

ner aluminiumwerkstätte in münchen sowie anderen unterstützern unseres lehrstuhls danken.

als lehrer ist es eine schöne erfahrung, zu beginn des semesters in ein meer von unbekannten gesichtern zu blicken, die studenten kennenzulernen und ihnen zu helfen, schneller zu lernen und zu begreifen, als sie gedacht hätten. einige kommen bei ihren untersuchungen zu höchst innovativen lösungen, die dann von der industrie weiterentwickelt und vermarktet werden. das alles wäre nicht möglich ohne die grossartige unterstützung eines teams von enthusiastischen assistenten, die den grossteil ihrer zeit in den dienst von lehre und forschung stellen und nebenher ihre eigenen projekte als architekten verwirklichen.

richard horden

team

microarchitecture / mikroarchitektur

a fascination for the beauty of nature, and the elegance and lightness with which aeroplanes and yachts move through the air, wind and water, are the distinguishing features of richard horden's activities as an architect and teacher.

his work on experimental microarchitecture projects is inspired by the wish for a direct experience of nature. his consistent reduction of weight and materials in his projects results in objects that are closer to the products of vehicle manufacture, aviation and astronautics than to architecture in the classical sense. technology transfer of this kind can be seen in the skihaus and point lookout projects. these small, independent prototypes provide a means of developing and testing lightweight building concepts for future-orientated forms of construction.

the examples of microarchitecture are light, modular, demountable, transportable, mobile, adaptable, self-supporting and recyclable. they permit an experience of nature with-

die faszinierende schönheit der natur und die eleganz und leichtigkeit, mit der sich flugzeuge und segelyachten in luft, wind und wasser bewegen, prägen die tätigkeit richard hordens als architekt und lehrer.

der wunsch, die natur unmittelbar zu erleben, inspiriert ihn zur arbeit an exporimentellen 'mikroarchitektur'-projekten. das konsequente reduzieren von gewicht und material führt zu objekten, deren nähe zum fahrzeugbau und der luft- und raumfahrt oft ausgeprägter ist, als zur architektur im 'klassischen sinne'. dieser technologietransfer zeigt sich in skihaus und point lookout. es sind kleine, eigenständige prototypen, mit denen leichtbaukonzepte für zukunftsorientiertes bauen entwickelt und erprobt werden.

mikroarchitekturen sind leicht, modular, zerlegbar, transportabel, beweglich, adaptiv, selbstversorgend und wiederverwertbar. sie ermöglichen ein naturerlebnis, ohne sie auf dauer zu beeinträchtigen – der leitsatz 'touch the earth lightly' drückt dies

skihaus was designed using aerodynamic principles for fast helicopter delivery (left).

point lookout on frazer island, australia; students before the assembly (opposite page)

skihaus wurde nach aerodynamischen gesichtspunkten für den schnellen helikoptertransport entworfen (links).

point lookout auf frazer island, australien ; studenten vor der montage (gegenüber).

'touch the earth lightly' — expressed by the image of a climbing child keeping clear space between body and mountain

'berühre die erde sanft' — ausgedrückt durch ein kletterndes kind mit deutlichem abstand zwischen fels und körper

out inflicting any lasting injury on it. this philosophy is expressed in the guiding principle: 'touch the earth lightly'. both projects, skihaus and point lookout, are mobile, require no foundations and leave no trace behind after they have been dismantled.

since the beginning of richard horden's teaching activities at the tu-münchen, a series of student projects have been realized as part of a programme of 'microarchitecture studies'. these study projects investigate the application of new architectural concepts, technologies and materials, from the initial design concept to the creation of the prototype.

microarchitecture allows students not only to design an object, but to pursue it through the entire process of development to its realisation. from the first sketch to the insertion of the last screw in the installation of their objects on site, students are encouraged to take responsibility for their projects and to keep track of their development.

aus. beide projekte, skihaus und point lookout, sind mobil, benötigen keine fundamente und hinterlassen nach dem abbau keine spuren.

seit beginn der lehrtätigkeit von richard horden an der tu-münchen sind in der reihe 'micro architecture studies' studienarbeiten entstanden, die vom entwurfskonzept bis zum prototyp die anwendung neuer architektonischer konzepte, technologien und materialien untersuchen.

die mikroarchitektur ermöglicht den studenten, nicht nur den entwurf, sondern den gesamten entwicklungs- und realisierungsprozess zu durchlaufen. sie werden ermutigt und aufgefordert, von der ersten skizze bis zur letzten schraube bei der installation vor ort die kontrolle über ihr projekt zu übernehmen und den überblick zu bewahren.

die oft sport- und freizeitbezogenen themen helfen den studierenden bei der identifikation mit dem projekt und vermitteln ihnen, dass architektur in allen phasen des pla-

shape of a bmw-roof as a reference for microarchitecture projects

die form eines bmw-autodachs als referenzbild für micro-architecture projekte

the subjects chosen are often related to sport and leisure activities, which helps students to identify with their projects and shows them that architecture can be fun at all stages of the planning process. to counter the erroneous belief that a strict separation of work and pleasure is necessary for a good architectural training, we quote the words of the architect and designer charles eames, who said: 'we take our pleasures seriously'.

prospective architects are systematically guided through the planning and construction process. working with references from other disciplines encourages lateral thinking. the analysis of the spatial situation and the time scale of a building assignment are followed by the precise formulation of a design concept, which then forms the basis for all necessary design decisions down to the actual execution of the work.

from the very beginning of a design, richard horden attaches great importance to a professional attitude.

nungsprozesses spass machen kann. dem vorurteil, dass eine strikte trennung von arbeit und vergnügen für eine gute ausbildung von architekturstudenten notwendig ist, stellen wir die aussage des architekten und designers charles eames entgegen: 'we take our pleasures seriously'.

systematisch werden die angehenden architekten durch den planungs- und bauprozess geführt. das arbeiten mit referenzbildern aus anderen fachgebieten fördert laterales denken. der analyse der räumlichen situation und des zeitlichen kontextes der bauaufgabe folgt das präzise formulieren eines entwurfskonzeptes, das die grundlage für alle notwendigen designentscheidungen bis hin zur ausführung bildet. richard horden legt von beginn des entwurfs an grossen wert auf professionalität. entwurfssystematik, aber auch die darstellung aller projektphasen in skizzen, plänen, bildern und modellen fordern die studenten. sie lernen

fisch haus form develops from car aerodynamics.

fisch haus ist in anlehnung an die aerodynamische form von autos entstanden.

'bergwald-spinne'

a systematic approach to design and the need to represent all phases of a project in sketches, plans, pictures and models represent a challenge to students. they learn to work quickly, precisely and with an eye to reality: 'this can be done faster and better'.

enthusiasm and an intensive process of guidance and supervision by the team, including the project assistants, are a tremendous spur for the students. this attitude is reflected in the sentiment that 'the students are our vips', expressed by richard horden on the occasion of a visit by the president of the association of german architects (bda). late-night corrections made on the train to the airport and faxes sent from london rha office about student projects are not uncommon.

all stages of the design process are tested by means of models, which may be built up to full size. richard horden frequently asks: 'how much does your building weigh?', which animates the students to use the new-

schnell, präzise und realitätsorientiert zu arbeiten: 'this can be done faster and better'.

enthusiasmus und die intensive betreuung durch das gesamte lehrstuhlteam bzw. die projektassistenten tragen enorm zur motivation der studenten bei. der satz 'students are our vips', von richard horden anlässlich eines besuchs des bda-präsidenten ausgesprochen, spiegelt diese einstellung wider. spätabends korrekturen in der s-bahn zum flughafen und faxe zu studentenprojekten aus dem londoner büro sind keine seltenheit.

alle schritte des entwurfsprozesses werden in modellen bis zum masstab 1:1 überprüft. häufig stellt richard horden die frage 'wieviel wiegt ihr gebäude?', was die studenten zur verwendung neuester leichtbautechnologie und -materialien animiert. diese vorgehensweise in der lehre erfordert eine realisierungsorientierte einstellung der universität, wo werkstätten genauso wichtig sind wie hörsäle und studios, aber auch die

silva spider, designed for accommodation in gorges, is one of the 'spider studies'.

silva spider, entwickelt zum aufenthalt in schluchten, ist eine von mehreren 'spinnen'-studien.

student richard schindler in the workshop of alu-meier, producing aluminium junctions.

der student richard schindler fertigt aluminiumknoten in der werkstatt von alu-meier.

est lightweight construction technology and materials. this approach to teaching presupposes that the university accepts the realization of projects as something normal and regards workshops as just as important as lecture halls and studios. it also presupposes an interdisciplinary collaboration with other faculties and industry.

students are encouraged to seek the cooperation of specialist engineers within the university and in private industry. this may relate to aspects such as structural engineering, aerodynamics, lighting technology or the optimization of energy use; or it can involve the patenting of ideas. the close collaboration with trade and industry affords students access to an enormous body of information in respect of materials, details and the execution of work, as well as experience in dealing with all those involved in the building process. in this way, students gain confidence in their ability to generate, realize and market a project.

interdisziplinäre zusammenarbeit mit anderen fachbereichen und der industrie.

die studierenden werden ermutigt, gezielt die kooperation mit fachingenieuren an der tu-münchen und aus der freien industrie zu suchen. dies kann aspekte der statik, aerodynamik, lichttechnik oder energieoptimierung, aber auch die patentierung ihrer idee betreffen. die enge zusammenarbeit mit handwerk und industrie bringt für die studenten ein enormes wissen bezüglich material, detail und ausführung, aber auch über den umgang mit allen am bau beteiligten. sie gewinnen vertrauen in ihre fähigkeiten, ein projekt zu generieren, zu realisieren und zu vermarkten.

sowohl die ziele der 'mikroarchitektur', als auch die vorgehensweise in der lehre sind übertragbar auf grossformatige projekte, wie die studienarbeiten 'lakeside apartments' und 'fire station' zeigen. beim bauen für das dritte jahrtausend geht es schliesslich darum, mit hilfe leichter,

extreme wind conditions were simulated with the beach point model in the wind tunnel (left).

extreme windverhältnisse wurden am beach point-modell im windkanal getestet (links).

paraglider in the sky (opposite page).
paraglider am himmel (gegenüber).

the aims of microarchitecture and this approach to teaching are also applicable to large-scale schemes, as the student projects 'waterspirit' and 'fire station' show. building for the third millennium implies reducing the burden on the environment with the help of lightweight, minimized forms of architecture. at the centre of these endeavours is the wish to improve the conditions of human life and to promote a state of co-existence between man, nature and technology.

claudia pöppel

minimierter architekturen die belastungen für die umwelt zu reduzieren. im mittelpunkt steht die verbesserung des lebensumfeldes der menschen und das miteinander von mensch, natur und technik.

claudia pöppel

richard horden (bottom) and claudia pöppel (below) in a final presentation.

richard horden (ganz unten) und claudia pöppel (unten) bei einer schlusspräsentation.

beach point

project:	munich 1997
location:	walchensee, germany
	laguna beach, california, usa
students:	jürgen schubert
	thorsten schwabe
	peter zimmer
	with markus kottermair
internet:	www.microsystems.de
coaching:	lydia haack
engineering:	tim brengelmann, dept. for structural design,
	prof. r. barthel, tu-münchen
aerodynamics:	albert pernpeintner, dept. for fluid mechanics,
	prof. b. laschka, tu-münchen
sponsorship:	windsurfing chiemsee, grabenstätt
	alu meier, munich
	alu suisse, singen
	zoche, munich
	bso, allersberg
dimension (lwh):	4.30 x 4.80 x 10 m
weight:	180 kg
rights:	protected registered design

beach point is a mobile observation tower with a deck and two elevated seats. the idea is based on existing rescue stations on the bavarian mountain lakes and a development of point lookout. the finished structure has found its way as far as the beaches of california. all components are limited to a maximum length of four metres and a maximum total weight of 180 kg. packed in three boxes, they can be carried by two people to relatively inaccessible locations. simple connections, based on boat construction details, allow the structure to be quickly assembled. the need for great stability even under extreme wind conditions necessitated comprehensive wind-tunnel tests, on which the structural calculations were based. motivated by the success of this project, the students set up their own design office under the name 'microsystems'.

beach point ist ein mobiler beobachtungsturm mit liegefläche und zwei hochsitzen. die idee entstand aus bestehenden rettungsstationen an den bayerischen bergseen bzw. als weiterentwicklung von point lookout. in seiner realisierung fand beach point seinen weg bis an die strände von kalifornien. alle bauteile sind auf längen bis zu vier meter und ein gesamtgewicht von maximal 180 kg begrenzt. sie können in drei transportboxen von zwei personen auch an unzugängliche standorte getragen werden. einfache verbindungspunkte, die sich an details aus dem bootsbau orientieren, ermöglichen eine schnelle montage. hohe anforderungen an die standsicherheit bei extremen windstärken erforderten umfangreiche windkanaluntersuchungen, die den statischen berechnungen zugrunde liegen. durch den erfolg des projektes motiviert, gründeten die studenten ihr eigenes designbüro 'microsystems'.

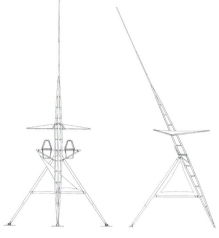

details of foot – *details fusspunkt*

above: details of the powder-coated aluminium structure with integrated canvas platform and sunshade sail
oben: die details zeigen die pulverbeschichtete aluminium-konstruktion mit sonnenschutz und liegefläche aus segeltuch.

right: students on the beach point during a press event on laguna beach, california
rechts: die studenten auf dem beach point während eines pressetermins am laguna beach in kalifornien

kayak club

project: munich 1997
location: river ammer, near saulgrub
students: jean-paul amato
johannes talhof
coaching: andreas vogler
materials: aluminium, htp-plastic
module (lwh): 4.20 x 4.40 x 3.35 m
dimension (lwh): 24.60 x 4.40 x 3.35 m

kayak club is a mobile club house for canoeists. it was developed for a well-known kayak course on the river ammer in the bavarian alps. the aluminium structure can also be used as a floating sales point or checkpoint during competitions.

the unit construction system is transported in a dismantled state in a set of floating containers, which also serve as floats for the aluminium structure and as moorings for the kayaks.

the kayak club can therefore be transported to locations that are accessible only by kayak, where it can be fixed in position and erected within only a few hours. the connections are designed as simple hinged joints, which create a flexible structure capable of adapting to the movement of the water.

kajak club ist ein mobiles clubhaus für kanuten und wurde für eine bekannte kajakstrecke an der ammer in den bayerischen alpen entwickelt. die aluminiumkonstruktion kann auch als schwimmender 'sales'- oder 'checkpoint' bei wettkämpfen verwendet werden.

komplett zerlegt wird das baukastensystem in einem set von schwimmenden behältern transportiert, die zusätzlich als schwimmer für die aluminiumkonstruktion und anlegestellen für die kajaks dienen.

der kajak club kann so auch an orten, die nur per kajak erreichbar sind, plaziert und innerhalb weniger stunden aufgebaut werden. die knotenpunkte bestehen aus einfachen gelenken und bilden eine flexible struktur, die sich den bewegungen des wassers anpasst.

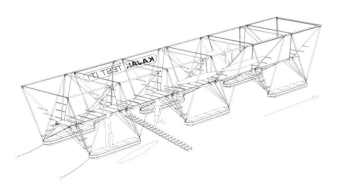

above: photomontage of the kayak club on the upper reaches of the river isar in upper bavaria.

oben: die fotomontage zeigt den kajak club am oberlauf der isar in oberbayern.

the structure was influenced by this cessna seaplane.

die konstruktion orientiert sich an diesem cessna wasserflugzeug.

cliffhanger

project: munich 1997
location: lake garda, italy
students: alexander felix
christopher von der howen
coaching: eva neumeyer
andreas vogler
engineering: tim brengelmann, dept. for structural design,
prof. r. barthel, tu-münchen
consultant: alu meier, munich
sponsorship: müller design technik, hardheim
beilken, lemwerder
materials: aluminium, canvas, plastic mesh sheet
dimension (lw): 4.10 x 3.38 m
weight: 36 kg

cliffhanger was designed as a plattform for surfers, yachtspeople and climbers on lake garda in italy, three hours by car south of munich. suspended only a few metres above the water it is conceived as a place for resting and sunbathing, and as an observation point for regattas.

the extreme location on a sheer rock wall as well as difficult conditions of transport and assembly necessitated a minimal, lightweight form of construction without any great technical elaboration. two tubular members are connected at one end to form a v-shape and are braced by two members that have the cross-section of a yacht mast. the structure is stayed by dyneema cables fixed to two pitons in the rock face.

a glass-fibre-reinforced synthetic mesh stretched between the tubes provides a deck for sitting and reclining. additional comfort is provided by a sunshade sail – which can be unfolded to form a tent – and by a sack for further equipment.

cliffhanger wurde als plattform tur surfer, segler und kletterer am gardasee in italien, drei autostunden südlich von münchen, entwickelt. er hängt nur wenige meter über dem wasser und ist als ort zum ausruhen, sonnenbaden und beobachten von regatten konzipiert.

der extreme standort an einer kletterwand sowie erschwerte transport- und montagebedingungen erfordern eine minimierte, leichte bauweise ohne hohen technischen aufwand: zwei rundrohre werden zu einem 'v' verbunden und mit zwei segelmastprofilen ausgesteift. an den knotenpunkten greifen dyneema-seile an, die das tragwerk zwischen zwei kletterhaken verspannen.

als sitz- und liegefläche wird ein glasfaserverstärktes kunststoffnetz straff zwischen rohre und masten gespannt. für zusätzlichen komfort sorgt ein sonnensegel, das sich zu einem zelt auseinanderfalten lässt, sowie eine packtasche für kleinteile.

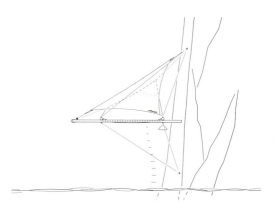

elevation
ansicht

above: the tubular aluminium structure is pre-assembled on the ground and then fixed to the rock face by a climber.

oben: die konstruktion aus alurohren wird am boden vormontiert und von einem kletterer an der steilwand befestigt.

right: cliffhanger affords a spectacular view over the water to the mountain panorama of lake garda.

rechts: cliffhanger bietet einen spektakulären blick auf das see- und bergpanorama des gardasees.

above: no sooner had the cliffhanger been fixed to the rock face than it attracted the interest of climbers.

oben: kaum war der cliffhanger an der felswand befestigt, erregte er das interesse der kletterer.

silva spider

project:	munich 1997
location:	partnachklamm, garmisch-partenkirchen
students:	jürgen amann
	thomas wenig
coaching:	andreas vogler
consultant:	tim brengelmann, dept. for structural design, prof. r. barthel, tu-münchen
materials:	aluminium, glass-reinforced plastic (grp)
dimension (lwh):	2.3 x 2.3 x 1.4 m
weight:	130 kg

spiders have conquered every corner of our planet. tremendously adaptable, they find a foothold everywhere, whether on their own legs or suspended in their self-built webs. this inspired the concept of the silva spider.

the aluminium structure, with three fully movable legs, is resolved into compression and tension members, in accordance with the principle of tensegrity. silva spider can, therefore, accommodate itself to any topography and will find a firm footing even in gorges and in gaps between buildings.

a glass-fibre-reinforced plastic cabin with a mouldable aluminium honeycomb core and acrylic glass window elements is inserted in the structure. in an open position, the flaps in the sides provide protection against the sun and afford an unimpeded view. a photovoltaic coating on the outside of the flaps generates energy for the cell.

spinnen haben jeden winkel unseres planeten erobert. sie sind enorm anpassungsfähig und können an jedem ort fuss fassen, ob auf eigenen beinen oder in ihrem selbstgeschaffenen netz hängend. davon inspiriert ist silva spider entstanden.

gemäss dem prinzip 'tensegrity' ist die aluminiumstruktur mit drei vollbeweglichen beinen, in druck- und zugelemente aufgelöst. silva spider kann sich so an jede topografie anpassen und findet selbst in schluchten oder baulücken sicheren halt.

in die konstruktion wird eine glasfaserverstärkte kunststoffkabine mit einem kern aus formbaren aluminiumwaben eingehängt, in die fensterelemente aus acrylglas integriert sind. an den seiten angeordnete klappen bieten im geöffneten zustand freie sicht und sonnenschutz. zur stromversorgung der kabine sind sie aussen zusätzlich mit einer photovoltaischen beschichtung versehen.

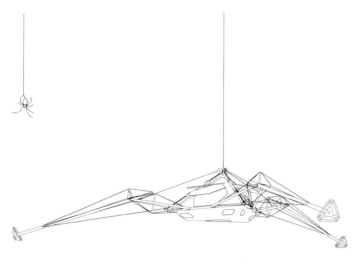

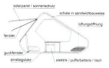

the 1:5 model, with a cabin for two people integrated into the tensegrity structure.
das 1:5 modell zeigt die in eine tensegrity-konstruktion integrierte kabine für zwei personen.

white water

project:	munich 1998
location:	river ammer, near saulgrub
students:	katrin doll
	sabine frohmader
	christina reschke
	claudia wieshuber
coaching:	craig synnestvedt
engineering:	tim brengelmann, dept. for structural design, prof. r. barthel, tu-münchen
material:	aluminium, canvas
dimension (lwh):	12 x 1.2 x 1.4 m
living area:	7.6 m^2
weight:	100 kg

the river ammer offers one of the most interesting stretches of white water for canoeists in the foothills of the bavarian alps. at one point, the rock walls on both sides form a natural gateway that leads to a long stretch of rapids, accessible only by kayak. the white water project highlights this special situation.

the narrows are spanned by a lightweight structure that acts as a bridge, as a viewing platform and as a place to spend the night. canoeists can pull their boats out of the water and climb up the rock face by means of metal rungs. a cable system fixed to the frame structure allows kayaks to be hung beneath the bridge. a set of sails can be unfolded if required to create a protected space in which to spend the night.

die ammer ist einer der interessantesten wildwasserbäche für kajakfahrer im bayerischen voralpenland. an einer stelle bilden die felswände ein natürliches tor zu einer langen wildwasserstrecke, die nur per kajak zugänglich ist. das projekt white water akzentuiert diese spezielle situation.

die schlucht wird mit einer leichten struktur überspannt, die als brücke, aussichtsplattform und zum übernachten dient. kajakfahrer können ihre kajaks aus dem wasser ziehen und an metallsprossen die felswand hochklettern. mit hilfe eines seilsystems in der rahmenstruktur, werden die kajaks hochgezogen und unter die brücke gehängt. ausfaltbare segel formen bei bedarf einen raum zum übernachten.

site plan
lageplan

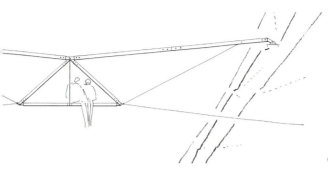

elevation
ansicht

simple pin-joint details facilitate easy assembly.

einfache bolzendetails erlauben eine unkomplizierte montage.

kayaks can be hung under the bridge.
kajaks werden unter die brücke gehängt.

the dramatically positioned structure sleeps two to three people.

die dramatisch plazierte konstruktion bietet platz für zwei bis drei personen.

air camp

project:	munich 1998
location:	nationalpark bayerischer wald
students:	julia haas
	andreas kienle
coaching:	eva neumeyer
	andreas vogler
consultant:	vilsmayer metallbau, pfakofen
sponsorship:	krah seilsicherungen, garmisch-partenkirchen
	vilsmayer metallbau, pfakofen
	w. junge sportartikelmarketing, witten
	mth zeltbau, schechingen
	ploch segelmacherei, münchen
materials:	aluminum, rip-stop nylon
dimension (lwh):	1.8 x 1.8 x 1.4 m
weight:	15 kg

air camp was designed as an observation point for a wildlife sanctuary in the bavarian forest. this modern tree house provides protection against animals in the park and can be used as a platform for wildlife photographers or for campers.

in its dismantled state, air camp can be carried in a rucksack by a single person and assembled with a minimum of effort. the platform consists of a square frame of aluminium tubes, between which a fabric base is spanned. it is braced by a three-dimensional structure of aluminium rods that also form a supporting framework for the tent skin. details and materials are based on high-tech developments in mountaineering equipment and hang-gliders.

air camp was presented to a broader public at the 'european outdoor fair 98' in friedrichshafen and at the 'caravan salon 98' in düsseldorf.

air camp ist als beobachtungsstation für ein naturschutzgebiet im bayerischen wald entstanden. das moderne baumhaus lässt sich als plattform für tierfotografen oder zum campen, geschützt vor tieren, einsetzen.

air camp kann zerlegt von einer person im rucksack getragen und mit minimalem aufwand aufgebaut werden. die konstruktion besteht aus einer quadratischen plattform aus aluminiumrohren, zwischen die ein textiler boden gespannt ist. eine dreidimensionale struktur aus aluminiumstäben dient zur aussteifung des bodens und bildet gleichzeitig die unterkonstruktion für die hülle. details und material orientieren sich an high-tech-entwicklungen aus dem bergsport und der konstruktion von deltaseglern.

air-camp wurde auf der 'europäischen outdoor messe 98' in friedrichshafen und dem 'caravan salon 98' in düsseldorf einer breiten öffentlichkeit vorgestellt.

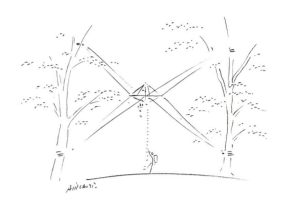

cable fixing to trees and aluminium frame on a scale 1:1

knotenpunkte in 1:1 zur befestigung der seile an baum und alurahmen

student andreas kienle high up in the tree tops

student andreas kienle hoch oben in den baumkronen

detail drawings
detailzeichnungen

boat house

project: munich 1997
location: kochelsee
students: christian ferber
thomas straub
coaching: claudia pöppel
materials: aluminium, plywood, foam insulation
module (lwh): 2.5 x 4.0 x 3.0 m
dimension (lwh): 32.5 x 2.5 x 3.0 m
weight module: 267 kg

the project was designed for a location not far from murnau, where the group of artists known as the 'blauer reiter' lived at the beginning of the 20th century. the cabins are meant to provide artists with an opportunity to draw inspiration from the wonderful natural landscape of this area.

in order to ensure that no traces were left behind on the sensitive shore of the kochelsee, a mobile, autonomous modular system was developed that can be used in other waterside situations as well. the entire components for one unit can be carried by two people. the modules are suspended in an aluminium frame, rather like boats in their dry berths in winter, and can be lined up additively to form an artists' colony. the individual cabins serve as sleeping quarters and as a shelter. service facilities are grouped together in a communal zone.

das projekt befindet sich in der umgebung von murnau, wo sich anfang des jahrhunderts die künstlergruppe 'der blaue reiter' formierte. die kabinen sollen künstlern gelegenheit geben, sich von der einzigartigen naturlandschaft inspirieren zu lassen.

um am sensiblen ufer des kochelsees keine spuren zu hinterlassen, wurde ein mobiles und autarkes modulsystem entwickelt, das auch an anderen situationen am wasser eingesetzt werden kann. alle einzelteile können von zwei personen getragen werden. die module werden wie boote im winterlager in einen aluminiumrahmen eingehängt und zur künstlerkolonie addiert. die einzelnen kabinen dienen als aufenthalts- und schlafbereich. die serviceeinrichtungen werden in der gemeinschaftszone zusammengefasst.

aero II, designed by manfred curry

aero II, entwickelt von manfred curry

wassily kandinsky: 'snow-covered trees in kochel'

wassily kandinsky: 'verschneite bäume in kochel'

view from the lake
ansicht vom see

the model shows the transition from land to water in the sensitive shore zone.

das modell zeigt den übergang von land zu wasser an der sensiblen uferzone.

the model (1:20) shows the access strip and the frame structure, which stands on broad footplates without foundations on the bed of the lake. the pivoting solar panels generate electricity and provide shading from the sun.

das 1:20 modell zeigt den zugangssteg und die rahmenkonstruktion, welche auf breiten fussplatten ohne fundamente auf dem seeboden lagert. die drehbar gelagerten solarpaneele dienen zur stromversorgung und als sonnenschutz.

the timber shell structure consists of shaped laminated plywood sections, as used in modern timber boatbuilding. the self-supporting shell comprises an inner and outer skin, with injected foamed insulation and bracing ribs.

die holzschalenkonstruktion besteht aus formverleimtem sperrholz, wie es im modernen holzbootsbau verwendet wird. innere und äussere schale bilden zusammen mit der eingeschäumten wärmedämmung und einer rippenkonstruktion die selbsttragende hülle.

bee house

project: munich 1998
location: olching, germany
students: bernhard nickel
with albert fahr
coaching: eva neumeyer
craig synnestvedt
sponsorship: schreinerei fahr, gröbenzell
otto wolff, plexiglas, munich
isofloc, hess lichtenau
materials: wood, metal, isofloc, plexiglas
dimension (lwh): 5 x 5 x 2.1 m
weight: 750 kg (140 kg/module)

honeycomb module
bienenwaben

the beehive is a fine example of a modular form of construction. both the natural honeycomb and the standardized beehive are based on a consistent repetition of micro-elements. this provided the inspiration for the development of a modular unit construction system in timber.

bee house consists of a skeleton frame of prefabricated columns and beams that form an extendable unit system. using various wall and roof panels – opaque and translucent – the degree of openness and the natural lighting internally can be controlled. a passive use of solar energy is also possible. with standardization and prefabrication of the construction components, the bee house system can be erected in a very short time and lends itself to production on a large scale.

das bienenhaus ist ein sehr gutes beispiel für modulare bauweise. von der bienenwabe über die standardisierten bienenkästen, basiert es konsequent auf einem vielfachen des kleinsten elements. dies lieferte die inspiration für die entwicklung eines modularen baukastensystems in holzbauweise.

bee house besteht aus einem skelett aus vorfabrizierten stützen und trägern, die ein einfach erweiterbares und elementiertes gebäude bilden. mit verschiedenen wand- bzw. transluzenten deckenpaneelen können öffnungsgrad und lichtsituation im innenraum variabel gesteuert und die sonneneinstrahlung passiv genutzt werden. das bee house-system kann durch standardisierung und vorfertigung der bauteile in kurzer zeit errichtet werden und eignet sich für eine serienfertigung.

computer-controlled produced connecting plates

cnc-gefertigte verbindungsbleche

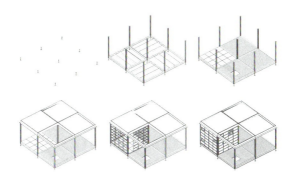

assembly sequence
aufbausequenz

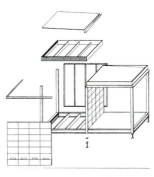

the bee house was built around
a tree in a garden outside

das bee house wurde in einem garten ausserhalb münchens um einen bestehenden baum errichtet.

exploded diagram of the
parts of bee house.

explosionszeichnung der bauteile des bee house.

weather station

project: munich 1998
location: latschenkopf
bad kissingen
students: arvid anger
markus brand
alexander groh
aleksandar milanovic
coaching: eva neumeyer
claudia pöppel
consultant: german meteorological office,
offenbach
materials: aluminium, foam insulation
floor area: 87.5 m²
costs: dm 250.000

in collaboration with the german meteorological service, a construction system was developed that can be easily adapted to various locations.

a raised platform, on which a series of prefabricated units can be placed, is erected on pad foundations. this simplifies the construction process on difficult sites and enables the station to be extended or relocated without difficulty. the shading provided to south face and roof considerably reduces the cooling load. depending on the location, solar collectors and wind-powered generators ensure independence of conventional energy supply systems.

in spite of positive reactions from the weather service, the local building authority refused permission for the implementation of the scheme at bad kissingen.

in koordination mit dem deutschen wetterdienst wurde ein bausystem entwickelt, das einfach an unterschiedliche standorte adaptiert werden kann.

punktfundamente tragen eine aufgeständerte plattform, auf der vorfabrizierte module plaziert werden. so wird der bauprozess bei schwierigem gelände vereinfacht und eine leichte erweiterbarkeit oder verlegung der station ermöglicht. die verschattung von südfassade und dach führt zur deutlichen reduzierung der kühllasten. je nach standort sorgen solarkollektoren bzw. windgeneratoren für eine unabhängigkeit von der herkömmlichen stromversorgung.

trotz positiver resonanz von seiten des wetterdienstes, stellte sich die zuständige baubehörde gegen eine realisierung des entwurfs.

at the german meteorological office, weather data of satellites and weather-stations are analysed.

beim deutschen wetterdienst werden wetterdaten von satelliten und messtationen verarbeitet.

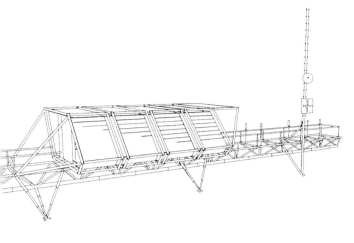

initially conceived for a mountain top, the design underwent further development for use in a flat area.

der zuerst für eine bergspitze konzipierte entwurf wurde später für eine anwendung im flachland weiterentwickelt.

facades are fully glazed for a better perception of landskape and sky.

vollverglaste aussenwandflächen ermöglichen den freien blick auf landschaft und himmel.

sky motel
brennerautobahn

project: munich 1998
location: griess, austria
students: rené thonfeld
christian weiss
coaching: siegfried lichtenauer
materials: steel, alum. sandwich elements
length: 120 m

autobahn viaducts in the alps afford magnificent views of vast mountain panoramas that car drivers are scarcely in a position to enjoy.

sky motel avails itself of the 78-metre-high brenner autobahn viaduct to make the tremendous view accessible both to travellers and to residents of the valley. the motel consists of a suspended lightweight structure with an additive linear arrangement of hotel units. the room cells are suspended in pairs from a central girder, which also accommodates the entire service runs.

a shuttle service conveys visitors from a parking area at one end of the bridge to the hotel lobby and restaurant. a lift links the facilities with the valley below.

autobahnbrücken in den alpen bieten eine wunderbare aussicht in ein weites gebirgspanorama, das leider von autofahrern kaum wahrgenommen werden kann.

sky motel macht sich die konstruktion einer existierenden 78 m hohen brücke der brennerautobahn zunutze, um reisenden und bewohnern des tals die grossartige aussicht zugänglich zu machen. es besteht aus einer abgehängten leichtbaukonstruktion mit linear gereihten hoteleinheiten. die raumzellen sind jeweils paarweise an einem zentralen träger aufgehängt, der auch den kompletten installationsstrang aufnimmt.

von einem parkplatz am anfang der brücke gelangt man per shuttle in die hotellobby und das restaurant. die verbindung zum tal wird durch einen aufzug hergestellt.

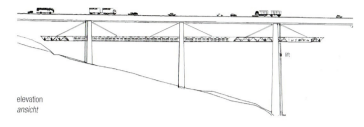

elevation
ansicht

the concept derives an additional use from existing engineering structures.

das konzept erschliesst die zusätzliche nutzung existierender ingenieursbauten.

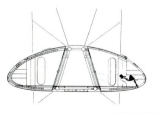

cross section
querschnitt

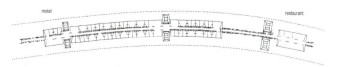

plan of entire development
grundriss gesamtanlage

lakeside apartments
rapperswil

project: munich 1998
location: rapperswil, switzerland
students: michael gerber
markus möslein
ralf weixler
coaching: lydia haack
andreas vogler
contact: planning department rapperswil
martin klöti
awards: 2nd prize
glaskon – archicad student competition
innovatives bauen mit glas

causeway

situated on lake zurich in switzerland, the town of rapperswil offers a breathtaking panoramic view of the glarus alps. a rail and road causeway built aross the lake at the beginning of the 20th century, however, disturbs the otherwise tranquil situation.

a development was drawn up, in consultation with the municipal building office, to provide this small community with additional residential accommodation and tax income. the proposals foresaw a continuation of the public promenade from the harbour to exploit the beautiful position on the lake and to create a built screen against noise disturbance. the carefully designed glass architecture provides a background in which the lake and the alps are reflected; and yachts can moor directly outside the hotel and the dwellings. the project has been exhibited in the town on several occasions.

die stadt rapperswil liegt direkt am zürichsee und blickt auf die atemberaubende alpensilhouette der glarner alpen. der am anfang dieses jahrhunderts gebaute bahn- und strassendamm quer über den see beeinträchtigt jedoch die sonst ruhige lage.

um der kleinen gemeinde zusätzlichen wohnraum und steuereinkünfte zu geben, wurde in zusammenarbeit mit dem stadtbauamt eine bebauung vorgeschlagen, die die öffentliche promenade vom rapperswiler hafen fortsetzt, die schöne lage erschliesst und gleichzeitig einen baulichen lärmschutz bietet. in der gezielt eingesetzten glasarchitektur spiegeln sich see und alpen. yachten können direkt am hotel und den apartments anlegen. das projekt wurde mehrfach in rapperswil ausgestellt.

elevation – ansicht

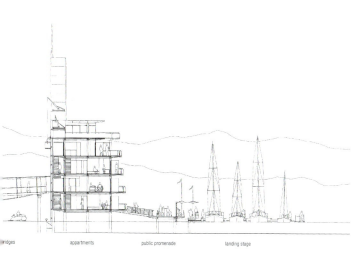

bridges | appartments | public promenade | landing stage

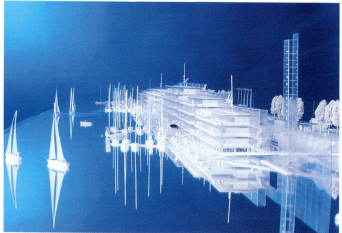

flats, hotel and casino are directly accessible by boat in a marina-like environment.

apartments, hotel und casino können wie bei einer marina direkt mit dem boot erreicht werden.

view of the glarus alps
ausblick auf glarner alpen

bridges connect the development to the causeway.

brücken erschliessen die bebauung vom seedamm.

fire station
expo 2000, hanover

project: munich 1999
students: rasmus dotzler
stefan lampersberger
coaching: lydia haack
awards: 1st prize in hebel student competition, bavaria

(our students won the top six places in this competition)

combining a fire station and police station, it is situated on a gently sloping site in hanover between the railway station and the main entrance to the expo 2000. the development comprises a hall for twelve fire engines and a police station, plus administration, leisure and rest facilities for the staff. a central feature of the design is the zoning into two distinct areas: a clearly visible area facing the expo entrance, containing the police station and the hall for the fire engines; and the private areas, which command a view to a quiet landscaped space.

the fire station is designed to allow an optimum sequence of operations without routes crossing. the transparent glass outer skin, into which photovoltaic elements are integrated, serves as a means of exploiting solar energy and at the same time lends the fire station the modern, high-tech image appropriate to an organization that will be constantly at the ready in the coming millennium.

die feuerwehrstation mit polizeiwache liegt auf einem leicht geneigten grundstück zwischen der s-bahn-haltestelle und dem haupteingang zur expo 2000 in hannover. sie beinhaltet eine halle für zwölf feuerwehrfahrzeuge und eine polizeiwache sowie verwaltungs-, aufenthalts- und ruheräume der einsatzkräfte.

kern des entwurfs ist eine klare zonierung in zwei bereiche: dem gut sichtbaren, zum expo-eingang im süden orientierten teil mit polizeiwache und feuerwehrfahrzeugen und dem privaten aufenthaltsbereich mit blick zur ruhigen grünanlage.

die feuerwehr ist auf einen optimalen, kreuzungsfreien einsatzablauf konzipiert. die transparente hülle aus glas mit integrierter photovoltaik dient der energiegewinnung und präsentiert die feuerwehr als moderne, hochtechnisierte und ständig einsatzbereite organisation für das nächste jahrtausend.

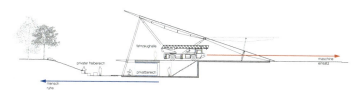

rest areas are situated beneath the vehicle level and are oriented to a peaceful leisure zone.

die ruheräume liegen unterhalb der fahrzeugebene und richten sich auf einen ruhigen freibereich.

front of building
frontansicht

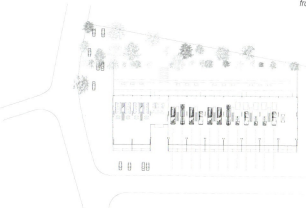

site plan
lageplan

glass exhibition centre
völklingen

project:	munich 1999
students:	dietmar geiselmann
	oliver schaeffer
coaching:	claudia pöppel
engineering:	annette koch, dept. for structural design,
	prof. r. barthel, tu-münchen
consultants:	prof. ch. bartenbach,
	k. ströbinger,
	bartenbach lichtlabor gmbh
	j. blumenberg, dept. for bioengineering,
	prof. e. winter, tu-münchen
	s. holst, transsolar, stuttgart
awards:	4th prize in
	dorma student competition 'steel + glass'

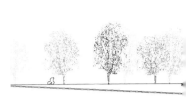

the glass exhibition centre is a competition design for the town of völklingen. the site is in the immediate vicinity of the 'völklinger hütte', a former steel works that was closed in 1986 and declared a world heritage site in 1994.

the design proposes the conversion of this disused industrial area into a landscape park and cultural centre, which presents the former works in a new light. the steel and glass conference centre is integrated into the landscape context of the scheme, but consciously seeks not to enter into any competition with the massive volumes of the industrial complex. only the glass roof, with its integrated shading elements, and the sloping landscaped area to the west are visible to the observer. changing weather and lighting conditions and cloud formations are perceptible in the internal space.

as example of pure surface architecture, the conference centre symbolizes the changes taking place in technology, with lightness and transparency representing the image of the future.

das glass exhibition centre ist ein wettbewerbsentwurf für die stadt völklingen. der standort befindet sich in unmittelbarer nähe zur 1986 stillgelegten und 1994 zum weltkulturerbe ernannten 'völklinger hütte'.

der entwurf schlägt eine nutzung der industriebrache als landschafts- und kulturpark vor, in dem sich die 'völklinger hütte' neu präsentiert. das konferenzzentrum aus stahl und glas integriert sich in diesen landschaftlichen kontext.

bewusst tritt es nicht in konkurrenz zu den mächtigen volumina der industriedenkmäler - einzig das gläserne dach mit integrierten verschattungselementen und die zur westseite geneigte grünfläche zeigen sich dem betrachter. lichtstimmungen, wetter und wolkenbilder sind im innenraum spürbar.

als reine oberflächenarchitektur symbolisiert das konferenzzentrum den wandel der technik - leichtigkeit und transparenz werden zum leitbild der zukunft.

cross-section
querschnitt

view over the glass roof
blick über das glasdach

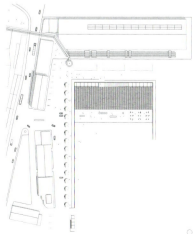

site plan
lageplan

lagoon exhibition centre
venice

project:	munich 1999
students:	peter hornung-sohner
	stephan ott
consultants:	città d'aqua, venice
	viviana ardone,
	consorzio venezia nuova
	de poli shipyard spa, pellestrina
engineering:	(foundations)
	mr. sobolevsky,
	huesker geosynthetics
material:	wooden sandwich panels
length:	180 m

inspired by the large number of islands of different shapes and character near venice, the lagoon exhibition centre creates a new independent space for art. it represents a visual sign and is, at the same time, an integral part of the landscape – a place of transitions in an environment subject to a constant process of change.

the form of the built structure is based on morphological investigations of the currents and interferes only minimally with the extremely sensitive ecological system of the lagoon.

the flowing transitions between inside and outside are echoed in the sequence of spaces within the building. ancillary rooms are added on the outside in the form of boxes raised above the water which also serve to brace the structure.

the building is used for exhibitions and research and can be reached in 15 minutes from venice by vaporetto. in its position and function, it supports the concept of a decentralized revitalization of the lagoon.

inspiriert von der vielzahl unterschiedlich ausgeformter inseltypen in der lagune von venedig, bildet das lagoon exhibition center einen neuen, eigenständigen 'kunstraum'. es ist visuelles zeichen und integrierter bestandteil der landschaft zugleich: ein ort der übergänge in einer umgebung ständiger veränderung.

die gebäudestruktur leitet sich aus morphologischen untersuchungen der strömungsverhältnisse ab und greift nur minimal in das äusserst sensible ökosystem der lagune ein.

übergänge zwischen innen- und aussenraum sind ebenso fliessend wie die raumfolgen im gebäudeinneren. nebenräume sind als boxen seitlich über das wasser geschoben und dienen gleichzeitig zur aussteifung.

das forschungs- und ausstellungsgebäude ist per vaporetto von venedig aus in 15 minuten zu erreichen und unterstützt durch seine lage und funktion die dezentrale wiederbelebung der lagune.

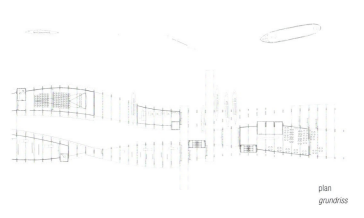

plan
grundriss

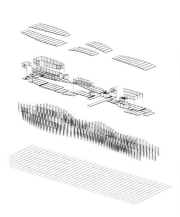

exploded diagram of the structural elements

die explosionszeichnung zeigt die strukturellen elemente des projektes.

the project reflects existing structures in the lagoon of venice.

das projekt orientiert sich an vorhandenen strukturen in der lagune von venedig.

energy tree
exhibition centre, munich

project: munich 1999
students: stefan bannert
 julia blees
coaching: eva neumeyer
 claudia pöppel
consultants: albert pernpeitner, dept. for fluid mechanics,
 prof. b. laschka, tu-münchen
 schindler aufzügefabrik gmbh
materials: steel, glass, aluminium, mylar
height: 300 m
Ø centre: 15 m
rights: patent pending

energy tree is a prototype for a 300-metre-high tower designed to exploit incidental wind loads over its entire height for the generation of energy.

the glazed core is supported by a tapering pentagonal truss that is visible on the outside. each of the horizontal rings fixed to the tower at 15-metre centres up its height is fitted with a rotor that turns horizontally about the axis of the building. attached to each of the rotors are five vertical aerofoil vanes, consisting of translucent mylar on a lightweight supporting structure. the construction allows views into and out of the building.

energy tree is conceived as a tower with a restaurant, hotel, conference centre and viewing platform for the trade fair site in munich.

energy tree ist der prototyp eines 300 m hohen turmes, der die über seine gesamte höhe anfallenden windkräfte zur energiegewinnung nutzt.

der verglaste kern wird von einem sich nach oben verjüngenden, fünfeckigen fachwerkträger getragen, der nach aussen sichtbar ist. im abstand von je 15 m trägt er einen ring, an dem sich ein rotor mit fünf vertikal befestigten rotorblättern horizontal um das gebäude dreht. sie bestehen aus transluzentem mylar auf einer leichten unterkonstruktion und lassen einblicke in das sowie aus dem gebäude zu.

energy tree ist als messeturm mit restaurant, hotel, tagungszentrum, bar und aussichtsplattform bei der messe in münchen konzipiert.

wind-tunnel tests were extremely successful and confirmed the anticipated efficiency of the system.

die windkanalversuche waren äusserst erfolgreich und bestätigten die erwartete effizienz des systems.

energy tree symbolizes the use of renewable energies.

energy tree symbolisiert deutlich die nutzung regenerativer energien.

isar tower
deutsches museum, munich

project:	munich 1998
students:	günter kober
	martin lechner
	michael schobert
coaching:	lydia haack
	andreas vogler
consultants:	tim brengelmann, dept. for structural design,
	prof. r. barthel, tu-münchen
	prof. r. junge, department for computer-aided architectural design, tu-münchen
	schindler aufzügefabrik gmbh
height:	177 m
internet:	http://vogon.caad.arch.tu-muenchen.de/m/prj/dtmuseum/doc/start.htm

the isar tower is conceived as an extension of the deutsches museum in munich. in its directional form, the tower is oriented to the south, to the river meadows and the alps.

it symbolizes the technological reputation of the museum and establishes a main entrance from the south, which has not existed up to now. express lifts serve the arrival platform in the middle, from where visitors disperse to the various exhibition levels.

one of the distinguishing features of the tower is its slenderly dimensioned load-bearing structure, which ensures a high degree of transparency. the floors are suspended from the main structure, so that load-bearing walls and columns are unnecessary. all facades and partitions are in glass, which affords an unimpeded view through the entire tower towards the mountains.

der isarturm ist als erweiterung des deutschen museums in münchen konzipiert. seine gerichtete form orientiert sich nach süden zu den isarauen und den alpen.

der turm symbolisiert den technologischen anspruch des museums und bildet den bislang fehlenden haupteingang süd. expressaufzüge bedienen die ankunftsebene in der mitte, von dort verteilen sich die besucher auf die ausstellungsebenen.

charakteristisch ist das tragwerk, mit dem ein höchstmass an transparenz erzielt wird. die geschossdecken sind von der hauptstruktur abgehängt, tragende wände und stützen sind nicht notwendig. sämtliche fassaden und zwischenwände sind aus glas, so dass man durch den turm hindurch die berge sehen kann.

plan
grundriss

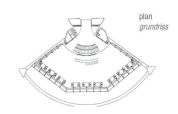

the tower is oriented to the south and forms an urban landmark that is visible from afar for one of the greatest museums of technology in the world.

der turm ist nach süden orientiert und bildet einen weit sichtbaren städtebaulichen akzent für eines der grössten technischen museen der welt.

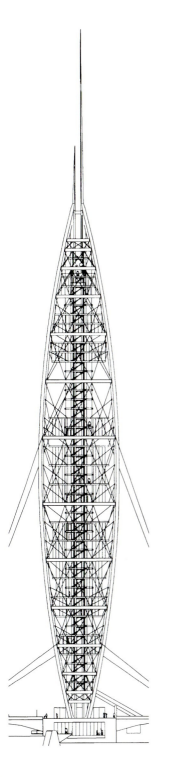

airship tower
friedrichshafen

project:	munich 1998
students:	stefan brunner
	birgit kuhn
	ekkehard riegel
	oliver zimmermann
coaching:	lydia haack
engineering:	tim brengelmann, dept. for structural design, prof. r. barthel, tu-münchen
consultants:	prof. t. bock, dept. for building realization and informatics, tu-münchen
	schindler aufzügefabrik gmbh
height:	377 m
weight:	7000 t

airship tower revives friedrichshafen's tradition as the cradle of airship travel. the form of the structure is reminiscent of a zeppelin. at the tip of the tower is a docking station that allows passengers to board modern airships. the project, combined with a yachting marina, is seen as a means of revamping the lakeside promenade with its harbour and zeppelin museum.

the structure consists of a mast stabilized by three fish-belly girders and cable stays. various cells containing flats, hotel rooms and conference facilities can be suspended within this main load-bearing structure.

vertical circulation is via cable cars, which ascend from the shore promenade to two distribution levels. from here, internal lifts provide access to the other levels. this enabled the tower to be designed with a minimum base area, so that the structure seems scarcely to touch the water.

der airship tower knüpft an die geschichte friedrichshafens als geburtsstätte der luftschifffahrt an. die gebäudeform erinnert an einen zeppelin. eine andockstation an der turmspitze ermöglicht passagierverkehr für moderne luftschiffe. das projekt mit zugehörigem yachthafen soll die seepromenade mit hafen und zeppelinmuseum aufwerten.

die konstruktion besteht aus einem abgespannten mast, der mit drei fischbauchträgern stabilisiert wird. in dieses haupttragwerk werden unterschiedliche module wie apartments, hotel und konferenzzentrum eingehängt.

die vertikale erschliessung erfolgt mit seilbahnen, die von der uferpromenade ausgehend in zwei verteilerebenen mit internen aufzügen enden. dies ermöglicht einen minimalen fusspunkt, so daß der turm die wasseroberfläche kaum zu berühren scheint.

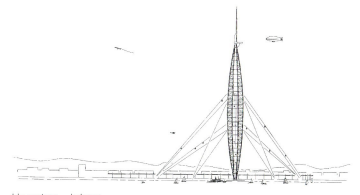

lake constance – bodensee

the airship tower forms the centre of a redesigned lakeside promenade in friedrichshafen on lake constance.

der airship tower bildet den mittelpunkt einer neugestalteten uferpromenade in friedrichshafen.

plan of distribution level *grundriss verteilerebene*

k1
site free

project: zurich 1993
design team: jan dvorak
richard horden
sarah kirby
andreas vogler
engineering: peter heppel
ludwig ilg
prof. klaus daniels
consultant: schindler aufzügefabrik gmbh
models: amalgam

k1 is a project for a 1000-metre-high skyscraper that is not constructed on a solid base from the bottom up, but aspires towards the sky in as light a form as possible. as part of a workshop at the eth zurich, a new architectural language for vertical sky structures and structurally efficient building forms was investigated.

with the support of peter heppel and ludwig ilg, the students investigated frisbee forms that offer a minimum of air resistance and where the airflow over all faces leads to uplift on the lee side. in collaboration with professor klaus daniels, all service systems were investigated. the giant redwood tree was taken as a point of reference. in the upper part of these trees, where capillary forces are no longer active, there is a direct water and energy gain.

one common problem in high-rise blocks is that lifts may occupy up to 80 percent of the ground floor area. this was overcome by providing direct access via airships and via cable cars that travel along the cable stays.

k1 ist ein projekt für einen 1000 m hohen wolkenkratzer, der sich nicht von unten her aufbaut, sondern so leicht wie möglich in den himmel gebaut wird. im rahmen eines workshops an der eth zürich wurden eine neue architektursprache und statisch wirksame gebäudeformen untersucht.

die studenten prüften mit peter heppel und ludwig ilg frisbeeformen mit minimalem luftwiderstand, die, allseitig umströmt, auftrieb an der leeseite erzeugen. zusammen mit professor klaus daniels wurden alle versorgungsströme untersucht. als referenz diente ein mammutbaum, der im oberen teil, wo die kapillarkraft nicht mehr wirkt, über direkte wasser- und energiegewinnung verfügt. dem problem, dass die aufzüge bei hochhäusern bis zu 80 prozent der erdgeschossfläche beanspruchen, wurde durch eine direkte erschliessung mit luftschiffen und seilbahnen entlang der abspannkabel begegnet.

living with great differences of altitude is an everyday experience in the alps. the cable car up the zugspitze takes only 10 minutes to cover the 2,000-metre height difference.

das leben mit grossen höhenunterschieden gehört in den alpen zum alltag. die zugspitz-seilbahn benötigt für eine höhendifferenz von 2000 m nur 10 Minuten.

reference

circulation

structure

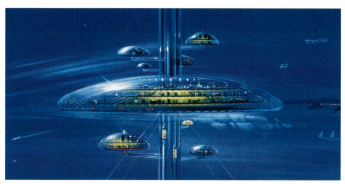

k1 — a study of high-altitude spaces

k1 — studie von räumen in grosser höhe

cloud formation over zermatt — natural aerodynamic architecture

wolkenformation über zermatt — eine natürliche aerodynamische architektur

wind-tunnel test at the institute for aerodynamics, eth zurich

windkanalversuch im institut für fluiddynamik an der eth zürich

light

light and nature

considerations:
solar
airflow
aerodynamics
sonics
thermal
pressure
precipitation
condensation
permeability
reflectivity
view
glare
light-day
light-night
light-colour
light-shade

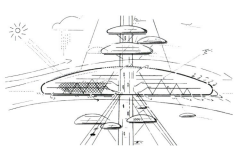

light

light and technology

considerations:
access and safety
maintenance
materials
structure active and passive
construction methods
weight distribution
building mobility
fluids systems
air/ gas systems
sonics
convection
electrical, electromagnetics
communications
adaptability
retraction
comfort
personnel movement systems
freight handling
waste, recyclability
exhaust and intakes

vienna fisch haus
mobile

project:	vienna 1996	chair:	prof. helmut richter
students:	gerhard abel		university of technology vienna
	ursula hammerschick	coaching:	willi frötscher
	silvia hörndl		anne wagner
	martin janecek		andreas vogler
	birgitta kunsch	materials:	aluminium, carbon fibre, foam
	paul linsbauer	weight:	45 kg
	christopher lottersberger		
	michael quixtner		
	magrit rammer		
	hannes schillinger		
	sakura watanabe		

the bivouac, named fisch haus has its inspiration from the traditional fishing huts on the banks of the river danube close to vienna. the students designed and built radio controlled, illuminated working models and full size mock-ups in carbon fibre and aluminium for a prototype habitable car top cabin or bivouac for two – a 'cuddle cabin' weighing 45 kilos. it is powered from the car's systems and accessed through the car roof-light.

the fisch haus supporting legs can fold down allowing the car to move away. systems are then powered by solar panels and batteries. the project made full use of the excellent aerodynamic facilities and wind tunnels at the university of technology vienna.

vorbild für das fisch haus sind die fischerhütten am ufer der donau in der nähe von wien. die studenten entwarfen einen prototypen für ein zwei-personen-biwak fürs autodach. die 45 kg leichte 'kuschelkabine' wird durch die batterie des autos mit strom versorgt; der zugang erfolgt über das schiebedach. soll das auto weggefahren werden, kann man die beine des fisch haus herunterklappen und die stromversorgung auf solarpaneele und batterien umstellen.

die studenten bauten beleuchtete und ferngesteuerte arbeitsmodelle und 1:1 mock-ups aus kohlefaser und aluminium. bei den windkanaltests kam ihnen die ausgezeichnete ausstattung der technischen universität wien zugute.

fishing hut close to vienna
fischerhütte bei wien

elevation
seitenansicht

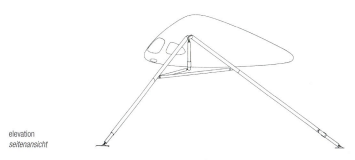

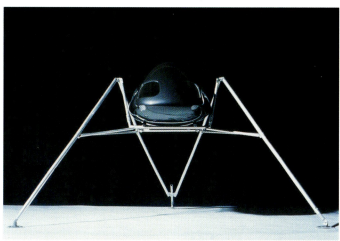

fisch haus is accessible by the car's rooflight and has its independent foldable supporting structure.

fisch haus wird durch das autoschiebedach erschlossen und kann unabhängig auf seiner faltbaren unterkonstruktion stehen.

1:5 model

detail of foot
fussdetail

solar spider
capri

project:	naples 1995
materials:	carbon fibre or moulded plywood, aluminium frame
support:	stainless steel wire rope, nylon
solar 'web':	flexible solar cells

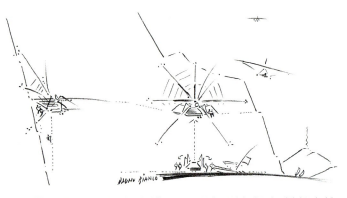

solar spider was conceived while initiating a workshop with the university in naples. it is a lightweight carbon-fibre cabin for 4-5 students, which can be temporarily attached to the cliffs of the island of capri using standard climbing equipment. the design is informed by the light construction of fisherman's huts to be found along the italian coast and will have total electronic self-sufficiency. the cabin will be watertight when closed and thus be able to float to the cliff, where it then can be installed. the exciting project would give a new micro-architectural dimension to the famous casa malaparte nearby!

solar spider ist eine leichte kohlefaserkabine für 4-5 studenten, die mit hilfe einer gewöhnlichen kletterausrüstung vorübergehend an den klippen der insel capri befestigt werden kann. inspiration für den entwurf des energieautarken gebäudes war die leichte bauweise der fischerhütten entlang der italienischen mittelmeerküste. die kabine ist in geschlossenem zustand wasserdicht und kann daher schwimmend zu ihrer klippe transportiert werden. dieses interessante projekt würde der berühmten, nahe gelegenen villa malaparte eine neue mikroarchitektonische dimension geben!

aluar
buenos aires

project:	buenos aires 1998
students:	lius aquili
	francisco cellini
	szu-ying lu
	fernanda punturo
	santiago reinhardt
	alejandro rodriguez
architects:	carolina isern
	corali taraciuk
	diego trolliet
consultants:	mederico faivre
sponsors:	georg freijo
	aluminium company of argentina
material:	aluminium frame

georg freijo, director of aluar, is a wonderful man and an inspiration to all who come close to him. a lover of art, architecture and innovation, he is supporting workshops in the use of aluminium and invited me to meet students at the uoa school in buenos aires. we used the four days to study a triangulared folding flood shelter 'project delta', an idea from diego trolliet.

the images show student fernanda punturo demonstrating the folding centre-pinned aluminium frame. we discussed how this could be used by aluar as a changing vertical feature, responding in height to wind forces.

georg freijo, direktor von aluar und förderer von kunst, architektur und innovativen projekten unterstützt workshops, die sich mit der verwendung von aluminium befassen. während eines viertägigen seminars entwickelten wir mit studenten der 'university of argentina' in buenos aires das project delta, eine dreieckige, zusammenfaltbare notunterkunft für überschwemmungsgebiete – eine idee von diego trolliet.

auf den bildern sieht man die studentin fernanda punturo beim auseinanderfalten des mittig verschraubten aluminiumrahmens, der als tragstruktur dient.

geodetic balloons
aberdeen and moscow

project:	aberdeen 1986
	moscow 1991
consultants:	kathy horden
	richard horden
	tony hunt
	robin webster
material:	melinex
dimension:	6 m diameter
weight:	100 gms

both moscow and aberdeen are located close to latitude 57°, so it is easy to understand that with the cold air temperature we could achieve elegant lightweight, flying geodetic structures (triangulated balloons). with a lot of energy and enthusiasm students in aberdeen built model-prototypes and drove to remote snowy hillsides to launch their architecture into bright, crystal-blue skies.

in moscow, students powered their balloons and spirits with vodka. a first vodka powered flight!

the purpose was to teach students geodetic construction and the importance of achieving more with less material, 'fun and function'.

moskau und aberdeen bieten mit ihrer kalten luft ideale voraussetzungen für ballonflüge.

in aberdeen bauten die studenten mit viel enthusiasmus elegante, leichte geodätische (auf dreiecksflächen aufgebaute) strukturen, um sie an abgelegenen, schneebedeckten hängen in den kristallblauen himmel steigen zu lassen. die moskauer studenten befeuerten ihre ballons wie auch ihre gute laune mit wodka: der erste wodkabetriebene flug!

ziel war, den studenten geodätisches konstruieren beizubringen und mit weniger material mehr zu erreichen: 'fun and function'.

balloons are first designed in stick form.
ballone werden zuerst in stabform entworfen.

kathy helps students tape the tetrahedron balloon.
kathy hilft studenten, den tetraeder zusammenzukleben.

flying tetrahedron structure
fliegender tatraeder

student florian fischötter with tony hunt and robin webster launching the largest balloon (above).
der student florian fischötter startet zusammen mit tony hunt und robin webster den grössten ballon (oben).

the taped melinex structures were flown on a cold winter day (right).
die aus melinex erstellten ballons wurden an einem kalten wintertag gestartet (rechts).

sport bridge
copenhagen

project:	copenhagen 1998
students:	søren aagaard
	susy carolin baasel
	gudrun holzer
	ng gin ling
	michael woodford
coaching:	andreas vogler
professors:	richard horden
	karin skousbøll
material:	aluminium

the brilliant work of american sculptor kenneth snelson inspired an intense and fascinating study into the construction of a tensegrity 'sport bridge' across the canals of copenhagen. the final design achieves a weight of approximately 1 ton.

we had worked with kenneth snelson – a student of buckminster fuller and in fact the real creator of the tensegrity principle or 'floating compression' – on a design for a tensegrity bridge across the thames.

this work has been an inspiration for most of our projects – since my first visit to one of his exhibitions in bryant park, new york in 1968.

the students worked intensely under the care of karin skousbøll and achieved a wonderful polished 1/20 scale model of the bridge.

das werk des amerikanischen bildhauers kenneth snelson war anlass zu einer faszinierenden studie für eine 'tensegrity' konstruktion über die kanäle von kopenhagen. die so entstandene sport bridge wiegt bei einer spannweite von 20 m ca. eine tonne.

bereits 1996 haben wir zusammen mit kenneth snelson eine fussgängerbrücke über die themse entworfen. der fuller-schüler und eigentliche erfinder des tensegrity- oder 'schwebender-druckstab'- prinzips hat mit seinen arbeiten die meisten unserer projekte inspiriert.

die studenten arbeiteten intensiv unter anleitung von karin skousbøll. das ergebnis war ein wunderbar poliertes 1:20 modell der brücke.

andreas vogler and kenneth snelson in the artist's studio in new york city.

andreas vogler und kenneth snelson im studio des künstlers in new york city.

1996 rha proposed a design together with kenneth snelson for a floating compression pedestrian bridge linking st paul's with the new tate gallery in london.

1996 schlug rha zusammen mit kenneth snelson eine 'floating compression' fussgängerbrücke vor, die st. pauls mit der neuen tate gallery in london verbindet.

professor karin skousbøll together with the students at the presentation of their design.

professor karin skousbøll zusammen mit den studenten bei der schlusspräsentation ihres entwurfes.

2nd year design lectures

winter lecture series

dimension
human scale
microarchitecture
houses 1 – 20th century
houses 2
zoning 1 – movement - circulation
zoning 2 – structure
zoning 3 – services
prefabrication
component design and assembly
modular building
urban design and waterfront building

summer lecture series

housing I
housing II
mixed use
cultural buildings
education
hospital
airports
commerce
industries
transportation

the teaching aim is to extend the range of the thought and design process. the design lectures begin with a definition of dimension – not only dimensions of length, width, height, but of surfaces, light, touch, colour, sound, energy, circulation. student architects learn to 'dimension' each of these criteria. in their studies they design and build models of the smallest elements: switches, doorhandles, lightweight cutlery and folding chairs.

the lectures illustrate aspects of scale from small components to houses and the evolution of 20th century housing in the winter term. important is the explanation of themes such as zoning, structure, services, prefabrication and component design. the summer term is an explanation of building types and categories such as schools, hospitals, industrial buildings, airports, etc. at the end of the summer semester, we visit the bmw pavillion at lenbachplatz in munich and discuss the lecture series in a café nearby.

mit der vorlesungsreihe 'gebäudelehre' im grundstudium wollen wir den gedanken- und entwurfshorizont der studenten erweitern. zuerst wird der begriff 'dimension' geklärt: dabei geht es nicht nur um länge, breite, höhe, sondern auch um licht, oberfläche, haptik, farbe, klang, energie und erschliessung. die studenten lernen, all diese dinge zu 'dimensionieren'. in übungen entwerfen und bauen sie modelle kleinster elemente: schalter, türklinken, leichtes besteck und klappstühle.

das wintersemester behandelt aspekte des masstabs, vom kleinen bauteil über einfamilienhäuser bis hin zur entwicklung des wohnungsbaus im 20. jahrhundert. wesentliche themen sind zonierung, tragwerk, haustechnik, vorfabrikation und modulares bauen. gebäudetypologien und -kategorien wie schulen, krankenhäuser, industriegebäude und flughäfen bestimmen die vorlesungen im sommer, die mit einem besuch im bmw-pavillon am lenbachplatz enden.

cutlery design by e. bodner and e. wolf (right)
besteckentwurf von e. bodner und e. wolf (rechts)

beach-chair by j. plötz and t. schlauersbach (below)
beach-chair von j. plötz und t. schlauersbach (unten)

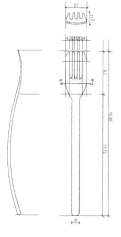

lightweight aluminium chairs by b. hahnel and th. gillich (right) and a. füssel and s. schwarz (far right).
leichte aluminiumstühle von b. hahnel und th. gillich (rechts) und a. füssel und s. schwarz (rechts aussen).

studies of knife, fork and spoon influenced the design by a. brückner and a. fthenakis.
studien von messer, gabel, löffel führten zum entwurf von a. brückner und a. fthenakis.

the crane in the lufthansa logo inspired the design of e. bodner and e. wolf.
der lufthansa-kranich inspirierte e. bodner und e. wolf bei ihrem entwurf.

microgravity projects
international space station

project:	munich 1998-2004	nasa team:	constance adams
students:	bianca artopé		david fitts
	björn bertheau		nathan moore
	brigitte borst		david ray
	thomas dirlich	engineer:	prof. e. igenbergs, dept. for
	julia habel		astronautics, tu-münchen
	claudia hertrich	consultant:	prof. h. baier, tu-münchen
	alexander hoffmann		prof. h. bubb, tu-münchen
	sandra hoffmann		reinhold ewald
	christian hooff		prof. h. hamacher, tu-münchen
	arne laub		hans huber
coaching:	lydia haack		ernst k. pfeiffer, keyser-threde
	claudia pöppel	funding:	bayern innovativ
	andreas vogler		bund der freunde der
			tu-münchen

In collaboration with the department for astronautics at the university of technology in munich and nasa's johnson space center in houston, our department has been conducting a number of microgravity projects since the autumn of 1998.

with the erection of the international space station, long-term stays in space will become a routine event. this poses the question of the habitable quality of a space station. the extreme demands made of astronauts require an ideal environment for work and relaxation. the main emphasis of the microgravity projects lies in the formulation of design criteria for the functional organization of workplaces and leisure areas in the international space station.

individual groups are drawing up proposals for standardized sanitary, sleeping and living racks within the habitation module. these proposals are being tested by means of full-size mock-ups. a presentation to nasa was so successful that they offered

in kooperation mit dem fachgebiet raumfahrttechnik der technischen universität münchen und dem johnson space center der nasa in houston laufen seit herbst 1998 'microgravity projects'.

mit errichtung der 'international space station' werden langzeitaufenthalte im all zum normalfall und es stellt sich die frage nach der aufenthaltsqualität einer raumstation. die hohen anforderungen an die astronauten erfordern eine optimale umgebung zum arbeiten und erholen. der schwerpunkt der 'microgravity projects' liegt im erarbeiten von entwurfskriterien für die arbeits- und aufenthaltsräume der internationalen raumstation.

einzelne studentengruppen erarbeiten vorschläge für die standardisierten sanitär-, schlaf- und aufenthaltsracks im habitationsmodul und überprüfen diese mit 1:1 mock-ups. eine präsentation bei der nasa war so erfolgreich, dass diese eine reihe von kc135 parabelflügen anbot, um

sponsors:
alu–meier, munich
brück leichtbautechnik, nister-möhrendorf
hans grohe, schiltach
horbach werbetechnik, munich
käthe kruse, donauwörth
rosner lacke, munich
schreinerei gleissner & stevens, munich
specken drumag, bad säckingen
vontana wasserbetten, oererckenschwig
many thanks, too, to all the unnamed supporters

iss-international space station

the neutral posture of the human body in a state of microgravity requires a redefinition of all design parameters.

die neutrale körperhaltung in der schwerelosigkeit erfordert eine neudefinition der entwurfs- und design-parameter.

building 9nw at johnson space center, houston: nasa engineer david ray conducts the munich space design group through the iss mockups.

gebäude 9nw im johnson space center, houston. nasa ingenieur david ray führt die munich space design group durch die iss mockups.

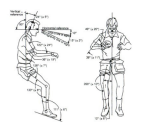

1:6 model of iss-crew-habitation module

1:6 modell des iss-aufenthaltsmoduls

to organize a series of kc135 parabolic flights to test the designs under conditions of microgravity.

the microgravity projects offer a splendid opportunity for a transdisciplinary collaboration between a wide range of experts as well as a cooperation with the space industry. exchanges with nasa are taking place via the internet and video conferencing. they provide an opportunity to plan in accordance with real needs and technologies. regular discussions with the german astronaut reinhold ewald reveal the user's point of view.

the synergetic potential of space architecture lies in a fundamental rethinking of the processes of planning and design under conditions of microgravity, and in becoming conversant with complex links between systems. the outcome is an enormous potential for new ideas and spin-off developments, which may also find an application in terrestrial architecture.

die entwürfe in der schwerelosigkeit zu testen.

die 'microgravity projects' bieten die möglichkeit einer interdisziplinären zusammenarbeit mit einer vielzahl von experten und der raumfahrtindustrie. der austausch mit der nasa über internet und videokonferenzen erlaubt uns, mit realen bedürfnissen und technologien zu planen. bei regelmässigen treffen gibt der deutsche astronaut reinhold ewald einblick in die situation des zukünftigen nutzers.

das planen und gestalten für die schwerelosigkeit führt zu einer völlig neuen betrachtungsweise von architektur. ausserdem zwingt es zur auseinandersetzung mit komplexen systemzusammenhängen. dadurch entsteht ein enormes potential für neue ideen und 'spin-off' entwicklungen, die ihre anwendung auch in der terrestrischen architektur finden können.

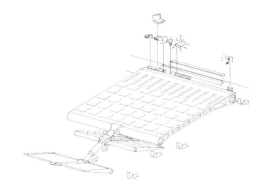

axonometrie of space-table-chair-module

axonometrie einer tisch-stuhl-einheit

wardroom-area with galley rack in hab module with modular table and fold out ovens (above).
küchen- und aufenthaltsbereich des hab-modules mit modularem tisch und ausfaltbaren öfen (oben).

test of the space-chair-table mock-up with simulated weightlessness in the swimming-pool (right).
mock-up der space-chair-table einheit im funktionstest unter simulierter schwerelosigkeit im swimming-pool (rechts).

hygiene rack
hygiene einheit

improvements to the department

project:	munich 1997
design team, tender and supervision:	richard horden lydia haack siegfried lichtenauer eva neumeyer claudia pöppel andreas vogler
building supervision:	building department, tu-münchen
sponsoring:	design funktion, munich erco, munich bulthaup, aich fröschl, munich dlw, bietigheim bissingen

the appointment of richard horden to a chair at the tu-münchen was the occasion for a conversion of the department's rooms. a modern, well-lit environment with transparent, open spaces was designed to stimulate the creative productivity of the team of students and tutorial staff and to lead to innovative design solutions.

a long, narrow undivided space offers all members of the team a view of the alps to the south. the entire furnishings are kept at a low height, thus enhancing the generous sense of space. the atmosphere is dominated by the white and pale grey of the furniture, carpeting, wall cupboards and aluminium sections, by the lighting concept and the numerous models.

this modern atmosphere extends through all the rooms of the department. the student workplaces are no different from that of richard horden. the standards set by the tutorial staff in their own work as architects communicate themselves to the students.

die berufung richard hordens an die tu-münchen war anlass für einen umbau der lehrstuhlräume. ein modernes, lichtes umfeld und transparente, offene räume fördern die kreative produktivität des teams aus studierenden und ihren betreuern und regen innovative entwurfslösungen an.

ein langgestreckter raum ohne zwischenwände im 4. obergeschoss bietet allen mitarbeitern den blick auf die alpen im süden. sämtliche möbel sind niedrig gehalten und betonen die grosszügigkeit des raums. die stimmung ist geprägt vom weiss und hellgrau der möbel, teppichböden und wandschränke, dem lichtkonzept sowie zahlreichen modellen.

diese moderne, helle atmosphäre zieht sich durch alle räume des lehrstuhls; die arbeitsplätze der studenten im studio unterscheiden sich nicht von dem richard hordens. der anspruch des lehrstuhlteams an die eigene arbeit als architekten überträgt sich auf die studierenden.

the department (above) offers views over munich and the alps. the design studio (below) during a student breakfast.

der lehrstuhl (oben) mit aussicht über münchen und auf die alpen. das design studio (unten) während eines studentenfrühstücks.

the design studio's interior design is the same as the departments. hang glider, models and prototypes serve as ongoing inspiration.

das design studio ist mit denselben möbeln wie der lehrstuhl eingerichtet. hangglider, modelle und prototypen dienen als laufende inspiration.

modular display system – main entrance
tu-münchen, visibility

project:	munich 1997-98
design team:	richard horden
	lydia haack
	michaela hoppe
	christopher von der howen
	eva neumeyer
	andreas vogler
lighting:	bartenbach lichtlabor gmbh
models:	markus möslein, peter trunzer
manufacturing:	alu-meier, munich
client:	tu-münchen

the development of a display system, together with the redesign of the entrance hall, a caad pool and exhibition space, is one of a series of projects undertaken by the department to improve the appearance of the tu-münchen. in addition to the need to meet functional requirements and to guarantee stability and reliability, the furniture system was to reflect the precision and aesthetics of modern engineering sciences. the design is based on a framework of anodized aluminium tubes, jointed with double-wedge connectors, and used in conjunction with aluminium composite panels. the furniture can be quickly assembled or dismantled by hand with a few basic tools, and can be stored in a space-saving form. the series comprises all units required for use in a modern university.

die entwicklung eines ausstellungssystems ist eines mehrerer projekte des lehrstuhls, die eine verbesserung des erscheinungsbildes der tu-münchen zum ziel haben. die möbel sollen alle anforderungen an funktion, stabilität und zuverlässigkeit erfüllen und dabei die präzision und ästhetik der modernen ingenieurwissenschaften widerspiegeln. sie basieren auf einer rahmenkonstruktion aus eloxierten aluminiumrohren, die mit doppel-keilverbindungen zusammengefügt werden. die paneele bestehen aus aluverbundplatten.

mit wenigen handgriffen und einfachem werkzeug lassen sich die möbel montieren, wieder zerlegen und platzsparend lagern. die serie beinhaltet alle module, die für den vielfältigen einsatz in einer modernen hochschule notwendig sind.

prototypes of exhibition panels (left), shelf unit and table (below)

prototypen der ausstellungspaneele (links), regal und tisch (unten)

the alusuisse alucore panels are held in place by the aluminium tubes. the system connection uses double wedges, like a handlebar of a bike.

die alukernpaneele von alusuisse werden mit rundprofilen fixiert. in den knotenpunkten stecken doppelkeilverbinder, wie in einem fahrradlenker.

detail foot
detail fusspunkt

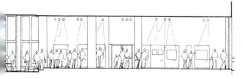

section through caad-centre, entrance and exhibition hall

schnitt durch caad-raum, eingangs- und ausstellungshalle

glass cubes project
tu-münchen, visibility

project:	munich 1998
design team:	richard horden
	eva neumeyer
	walter schwaiger
	andreas vogler
lighting:	bartenbach lichtlabor gmbh
models:	stefan lampersberger
	stephan ott

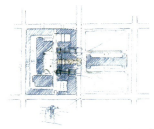

sketch site plan
skizze lageplan

the department made proposals for the redesign of the entrance area of the technical university. the building is situated in one of the most valuable museum districts in europe, and the project sought to mend an unfortunate piece of urban planning: the confrontation between the main entrance to the university and the end face of the alte pinakothek. further, the project intends to accentuate the entrance and to present the research activities to the outside world. an idea was developed in collaboration with the graphic artist walter schwaiger, according to which glazed cubes were to be inserted in the parking bays flanking the present entrance. these pavilions were to form new points of entry and also serve as exhibition spaces for the display of modern technology.

the light glass construction ensures a maximum degree of transparency in the two pavilions and also creates a welcome contrast to the solid walls of the existing structure.

im rahmen seiner untersuchungen zum erscheinungsbild der tu-münchen beschäftigt sich unser lehrstuhl mit der neugestaltung der eingangssituation. die tu befindet sich mitten in einem der hochwertigsten museumsquartiere europas. die städtebaulich unglückliche situation mit dem tu-haupteingang als direktes gegenüber zur stirnseite der alten pinakothek soll entschärft, die auffindbarkeit des eingangs erleichtert und die forschungstätigkeit der tu nach aussen dargestellt werden. zusammen mit dem grafiker walter schwaiger wurde die idee entwickelt, in den jetzigen parkbuchten seitlich des eingangs gläserne kuben zu plazieren. sie dienen als neue eingänge und gleichzeitig als ausstellungsfläche für moderne technologien.

die vorgesehene leichte glaskonstruktion ermöglicht eine grösstmögliche transparenz der beiden gebäude und bildet einen wohltuenden gegensatz zu den massiven mauern des altbaus.

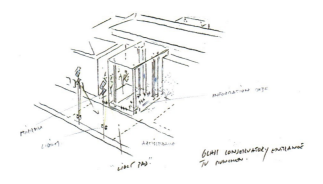

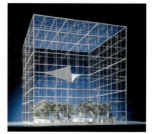

model views of the new transparent entrance cubes of the tu-münchen (top and above).

modellansichten eines neuen transparenten eingangs-kubus der tu-münchen (oben und ganz oben).

the glass cube project in stag place, london, was the inspiration for the entrance situation of the tu-münchen (above).

das 'glass cube' projekt am stag place in london diente als inspiration für die eingangssituation der tu-münchen (oben).

skydeck house

project:	england 1990
design team:	richard horden
	thomas höger
	sarah kirby
	oliver stirling
	michael wigginton
engineering:	ove arup and partners
	jack zunz
	jourdan engineering
costs:	davis langdon and everest
model:	amalgam

'the house as a lifestyle product' formed the motto for the skydeck project, which richard horden designed in 1990. this prepared the ground for the research into the 'smart house' in cooperation with the ofra systembau company.

compared with other sectors of industry, such as automobile production, the degree of prefabrication in building is very low. the advantages of prefabricated building components range from a reduction of the energy input and a minimized use of materials to the installation of intelligent service and control systems in buildings. a clear basic concept, a high degree of flexibility and economic efficiency make modular methods of construction an interesting proposition in housing. aim of the research work is to assess the development potential of systems of this kind in the context of terrace housing. the investigations are concerned with specific user requirements, their effect on building concepts and layout typology.

smart haus

project:	munich 1999
research team:	lydia haack
	richard horden
	claudia pöppel
	michael schneider
	andreas vogler
client:	ofra systembau, beverungen

'das haus als lifestyle-produkt' – aus dieser idee heraus hat richard horden 1990 das projekt skydeck entwickelt – ein vorläufer für die forschungsarbeit am smart haus, die in kooperation mit der firma ofra systembau läuft.

verglichen mit anderen branchen wie der automobilindustrie, ist der vorfertigungsgrad im bauwesen extrem niedrig. hohe baukosten und lange bauzeiten sind die folge. die vorteile der vorfertigung von bauteilen reichen von der reduzierung des energieverbrauchs zu minimiertem materialeinsatz und intelligenten kreisläufen im gebäude. eine klare grundkonzeption, das hohe mass an flexibilität und die wirtschaftliche effizienz machen eine modulare bauweise für den wohnungsbau interessant. die forschungsarbeit soll das entwicklungspotential bei reihenhäusern aufzeigen. untersucht werden spezifische nutzeranforderungen und deren auswirkungen auf gebäudekonzeption und grundrisstypologie.

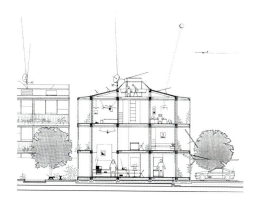

cross-section
querschnitt

assembly of the skydeck components
aufbau der skydeck-komponenten

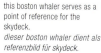

this boston whaler serves as a point of reference for the skydeck.
dieser boston whaler dient als referenzbild für skydeck.

in addition to conducting an intense investigation into ways of improving the production process, the skydeck study examined marketing concepts and the appearance of a modern modular housing system, which could be marketed like a car or yacht.

neben intensiven studien zur verbesserung des produktionsprozesses beleuchtete die skydeck studie auch die vermarktungskonzepte und das erscheinungsbild eines modernen modularen haussystems. es sollte wie ein modernes auto oder eine yacht vertrieben werden.

appendix

richard horden

1944	born in leominster, uk
1969	diploma at aa, london
1971	farrell grimshaw partnership
1972-75	spence & webster, london
1975-85	sir norman foster and partners (sainsbury centre, hongkong shanghai bank, stansted airport, etc.)
1985-	richard horden associates
1993	financial times award for architecture
1996-	professor at university of technology, munich

name index

london office

richard horden
raj a'suresh
sarah kirby
sarah forbes-waller
michael barth
barbara bouza
ken boyd
jill catling
claire cheney
david chipperfield
angelika class
alictair cook
diana cowley
bill cuneo
wendy dunning

jan dvorak
charles dymond
mira esposito
tobias fischer
florian fischötter
stuart forbes-waller
jean franco
elizabetta galimberti
alan grant
sarah harrison
ursula heinemann
caroline hislop
claudia hoge
thomas höger
tim hooson

kathy horden
peter horden
richard hywell-evans
russel jones
sabine kaufmann
brian kelly
wolfgang kessler
robert klashka
lars klatte
benjamin knight
silke krüger
billie lee
liu kee lee
eva martin
susan mclean

brian mcclymont
claudia mühlhoff
sarah north
louise peacocke
rawden pettit
dominic reid
dawn robertson
martina sedelmayer
ulrike seifritz
oliver stirling
henning stummel
kirstie tucker
andreas vogler
charles walker
paul warner

students

aagaard, søren 106
abel, gerhard 100
amann, jürgen 70
amato, jean-paul 66
anger, arvid 80
aquili, lius 103
artopé, bianca 110
baasel, susy c. 106
bannert, stefan 92
bertheau, björn 110
blees, julia 92
bodner, eva 109
borst, brigitte 110
brand, markus 80
brückner, astrid 109
brunner, stefan 96
cellini, francisco 103
dirlich, thomas 110
doll, katrin 72
dotzler, rasmus 86
fahr, albert 78
felix, alexander 68
ferber, christian 76
frohmader, sabine 72

fthenakis, alexander 109
füssel, andreas 109
geiselmann, dietmar 88
gerber, michael 84
gillich, thomas 109
groh, alexander 80
haas, julia 74
habel, julia 110
hahnel, barbara 109
hammerschick, ursula 100
hertrich, claudia 110
hoffmann, alex 110
hoffmann, sandra 110
holzer, gudrun 106
hooff, christian 110
hörndl, silvia 100
hornung-sohner, peter 90
howen, christopher 68
janecek, martin 100
kienle, andreas 74
kober, günter 94
kottermair, markus 64

kuhn, birgit 96
kunsch, birgitta 100
lampersberger, stefan 86
laub, arne 110
lechner, martin 94
ling, ng gin 106
linsbauer, paul 100
lottersberger, christopher 100
lu, szu-ying 103
milanovic, aleksandar 80
möslein, markus 84
nickel, bernhard 78
ott, stephan 90
plötz, jakob 109
punturo, fernanda 103
quixtner, michael 100
rammer, magrit 100
reinhardt, santiago 103
reschke, christina 72
riegel, ekkehard 96
rodriguez, alejandro 103

schaeffer, oliver 88
schillinger, hannes 100
schlauersbach, torsten 109
schobert, michael 94
schubert, jürgen 64
schwabe, thorsten 64
schwarz, sebastian 109
straub, thomas 76
talhof, johannes 66
thonfeld, rené 82
watanabe, sakura 100
weiss, christian 82
weixler, ralf 84
wenig, thomas 70
wolf, eva 109
woodford, michael 106
zimmer, peter 64
zimmermann, oliver 96
and others

department, tu-münchen

lydia haack

1983-88	studies at fh-münchen
1988-89	ralph+doris thut
1989-91	studies at aa, london
1989-95	michael hopkins + partners, london
1995-	teaching assistant of hermann schröder and richard horden
1995-	own office with john höpfner

siegfried lichtenauer

1977-80	draftsman
1986-93	studies at tu-münchen
1993 -95	hüther, hebensperger – hüther, röttig
1993-	own projects
1995-99	teaching assistant of hermann schröder and richard horden
1999	guest professor in huazhong, china

eva neumeyer

1984-94	studies at tu-münchen, tu-graz, akademie der bildenden künste munich
1992-93	fumihiko maki, munich
1994	otto steidle, munich, own projects
1996-	teaching assistant of richard horden
1997	förderpreis der stadt münchen

claudia pöppel

1985-91	studies at tu-kaiserslautern, tu-münchen
1991	sampo widmann, munich
1992-94	wagmann architekten, munich
1994-	teaching assistant of hermann schröder and richard horden
1997-	own office with jürgen thum

michael schneider

1991-98	studies at tu-münchen and rhode island school of design (risd), usa
1996	own projects
1997	heym, munich
1998	goergens + miklautz, munich
1998-	teaching assistant of richard horden

leslie stein

1988-97	studies at university of michigan
1992-94	fry & partners architects, michigan
1995-97	teaching assistant, univ. of michigan
1996	jourda & perraudin, lyon, france
1997-98	herzog+partner, munich
1998	teaching assistant of richard horden
1999-	nbbj, seattle, usa

thomas straub

1984-88	siemens ag, munich
1991-98	studies at tu-münchen
1995-99	herzog+partner, munich
1998-	own office, munich
1998-	projects and competitions with andreas vogler
1999-	teaching assistant of richard horden

craig synnestvedt

1989-96	studies at university of michigan
1992-94	construction experience, mkd development corp, seattle, usa
1995	albert kahn and assoc., detroit, usa
1996	r.u.a architects, prague
1997-98	teaching assistant of richard horden
1998-	mithun partners, seattle, usa

andreas vogler

1988-94	studies at eth zürich and rhode island school of design (risd)
1993	kozo systems inc., tokyo
1995-	associate at rha, london
1996-	teaching assistant of richard horden
1996-	own office, basel; projects and competitions with thomas straub

administration team

1996-97	andrea otto
1997-	alexandra v. petersdorff

photo index

2 niccolò baldassini; 4 r. horden; 6 rutan aircraft factory; 7 jan dvorak; 10.1 john donat; 10.2 bill bachmann; 12.1 ken kirkwood; 12.2 lufthansa; 12.3 kenneth snelson; 13 ken kirkwood; 14.1 alex kallenberger; 14.2-3 dennis gilbert/view; 14.4 bmw; 14.5 dennis gilbert/view; 15 john norris; 16 eamonn o'mahony; 17 vic carless; 18.1 r. horden; 18.2 ruedi hornberger; 19.1-4 r. horden; 19.5 eamonn o'mahony

architecture
all photographs by eamonn o'mahony, except:
20 r. horden; 22.1 r. horden; 22.2 billie lee; 29.1 peter stumpf; 29.2-3 dennis gilbert/view; 30 dennis gilbert/view; 31.1 dennis gilbert/view; 31.2-3 r. horden; 31.4 dennis gilbert/view; 34 billie lee; 35.1 billie lee; 35.2 r. horden; 45.1 r. horden; 45.2 richard davis; 45.3 r. horden; 47.1 r. horden; 47.2 jason hawkes; 51 louisa parry

teaching
all photographs by the respective students, except:
54.1 foto huber, garmisch; 55 flughafen münchen gmbh; 56.1 pat gallis; 56.2 microsystems; 57 ulrich benz; 58 alex kallenberger; 59.1 hans grossen; 59.2-3 r. horden; 60.1 bmw; 60.2 hannes schillinger; 61 jürgen amann; 62.1-62.2 ralf drewing; 62.3 microsystems; 63.1 lehrstuhl horden; 63.2 motorbuch verlag, stuttgart; 63.3 lehrstuhl horden; 65 pat gallis; 69.4-5 federico pedrotti; 73.2 craig synnestvedt; 75.1-2 craig synnestvedt; 75.3 ralf horstkotte; 76.1 lenbach haus, munich, vg bild kunst, bonn; 76.2 yacht, delius klasing verlag 80 deutscher wetterdienst; 82 tourismusverband griess; 85.1 craig synnestvedt; 85.2 ernst lininger; 85.3 craig synnestvedt; 87 albert scharger, ulrich benz; 89 franziska hasse; 92 peter thammer; 96 schwenk gmbh, haigerloch; 99.1 vic carless; 99.2-3 r. horden; 100 r. horden; 102 luciano d'angelo; 103.1-3 r. horden; 103.4-5 diego trolliet; 104-107 r. horden; 109 albert scharger; 110 r. horden; 111.1 nasa; 111.2 r. horden; 112, 113.1, 115.1 albert scharger, ulrich benz; 115.2 r. horden; 117.1,3 peter zimmer; 117.2, 4, 6 craig synnestvedt; 117.5 tom miller; 119.1 albert scharger, ulrich benz; 119.2 eamonn o'mahony; 119.3 albert scharger, ulrich benz; 121.1-2 tom miller; 121.3 boston whaler; 121.4 tom miller

appendix
124.1 eamonn o'mahonny; 124.2-3 lehrstuhl horden; 125 lehrstuhl horden; 128 dennis gilbert/view

in the case of certain illustrations, it was not possible to identify the copyright holders. persons owning copyrights are requested to contact the editor.

impressum

layout + cover design	richard horden christopher v. der howen claudia pöppel andreas vogler ralf weixler
typeset	helvetica light
contact	lehrstuhl für entwerfen und gebäudelehre, prof. richard horden arcisstrasse 21 d-80290 münchen sekr.horden@lrz.tu-muenchen.de

www.arch.tu-muenchen.de/light/

deutsche bibliothek cataloging-in-publication data

horden, richard:
richard horden – architecture and teaching: buildings, projects, microarchitecture workshops/ ed. by lehrstuhl für entwerfen und gebäudelehre prof. richard horden, tu-münchen. [transl. into engl.: peter green, andreas vogler. übers. ins dt.: enrica ferrucci, christopher v. der howen, barbara loreck, claudia pöppel, andreas vogler, ralf weixler]. – basel ; boston ; berlin : birkhäuser, 1999
isbn 3-7643-6152-2

this work is subject to copyright. all rights are reserved, whether the whole or part of the materials is concerned, specifically the rights of translation, reprinting, re-use of illustrations, recitation, broadcasting, reproduction on microfilms or in other ways, and storage in data banks. for any kind of use, permission of the copyright owner must be obtained.

©1999 birkhäuser – publishers for architecture
p.o. box 133, ch-4010 basel, switzerland.
printed on acid-free paper produced from chlorine-free pulp. tcfoo. printed in germany.
isbn 3-7643-6152-2
isbn 0-8176-6152-2

also available:

richard horden –
light tech
werner blaser (ed.)
1995 birkhäuser - publishers for architecture
isbn 3-7643-5220-5
isbn 0-8176-5220-5

acknowledgements

sponsors

this exhibiton and book have been made possible by the spontaneous generosity of sir robert and lady lisa sainsbury. of course, others have generously contributed much time and resources, but the first and largest donation was from the sainsburys, which gave confidence to our team of students and assistants to progress work for the opening in zurich on august 25th.
thank you sincerely, bob and lisa.

richard horden

robert and lisa sainsbury
allianz ag
alusuisse singen
bartenbach lichtlabor gmbh
brück leichtbautechnik
bund der freunde der tu-münchen
hl-technik ag
ofra systembau gmbh & co
sailer, stepan und partner ingenieure
schindler aufzügefabrik gmbh
siemens design und messe gmbh

book and exhibition team

andreas vogler, who also compiled 'light tech', and claudia pöppel have led our hard-working team of students, christopher v. der howen and ralf weixler, with characteristic charm and energy. as i write this, the computer hard disk drive with the book data has gone down and andreas determinedly sets to and dismembers the unfortunate machine. (21.6.99)
i would like to thank all my students for their participation and express my sincere thanks to all teaching assistants for their help and enthusiasm over the past three years.
thanks to you all.

richard horden

christopher v. der howen
claudia pöppel
torsten schlauersbach
manon stockhammer
andreas vogler
ralf weixler

lady sainsbury was a nurse and is now concerned to improve the quality of the medical environment in england. this glass patient lift in the sainsbury wing at hammersmith hospital has electronically controlled privacy glass.

lady sainsbury, die früher krankenschwester war, setzt sich für eine verbesserung der medizinischen versorgung in england ein. dieser lift im hammersmith hospial respektiert mit seinen elektrochromatischen gläsern die privatsphäre der patienten.